Contradictions & Contraceptions

Essays on Feminism and Social Justice

EMMA GOLDMAN

Contradictions & Contraceptions: Essays on Feminism and Social Justice
Copyright © 2025 by VertVolta Press
All rights reserved. Published in the United States by Vertvolta Press.
No part of this book's design may be reproduced in any manner whatsoever without prior written permission.

No AI Training: Without in any way limiting the publisher's exclusive rights under copyright, any use of this publication to "train" generative artificial intelligence (AI) technologies to generate text is expressly prohibited. The publisher reserves all rights to license uses of this work for generative AI training and development of machine learning language models.

Book and Cover Design: Vladimir Verano, VertVolta Design

Cover: © Victor Kitaykin via istockphoto.com

Introduction © 2025 Sarah Keliher

print ISBN: 978-1-60944-163-0

ebook ISBN: 978-1-60944-164-7

VERTVOLTA PRESS

Seattle, Washington

publisher@vertvoltapress.com www.vertvoltapress.com

- *i*   *Introduction - Sarah Keliher*

- *1*   *Marriage* - 1897

- *13*   *Child & Its Enemies* - 1916

- *29*   *Social Aspects of Birth Control* - 1916

- *45*   *Mary Wollstonecraft, Her Tragic Life and Her Passionate Struggle for Freedom* - 1911

- *65*   *Traffic in Women* - 1911

- *91*   *Woman Suffrage* - 1911

- *113*   *Tragedy of Woman's Emancipation* - 1911

- *131*   *Marriage and Love* - 1911

It has been said that nature uses a vast amount of human material to create one genius. The same holds good of the true rebel, the true pioneer. Mary was born and not made through this or that individual incident in her surroundings. The treasure of her soul, the wisdom of her life's philosophy, the depth of her World of thought, the intensity of her battle for human emancipation and especially her indomitable struggle for the liberation of her own sex, are even today so far ahead of the average grasp that we may indeed claim for her the rare exception which nature has created but once in a century.

Emma Goldman's words about Mary Wollstonecraft could just as easily be applied to her—so far ahead of the average grasp that she still seems in many ways far ahead today. She looked back on Wollstonecraft in much the same way we look back at her, finding inspiration in the lives of people who lived through hard, dark times without giving up their fight for liberation.

Goldman continues to be a source of inspiration for dreamers and leftists today, despite her flaws and blind spots, and despite her contradictions, all of which can be seen to some extent in the pieces contained here. Her vision of radical liberation brought her into conflict with left leaning thinkers who supported suffrage as well as with figures of the establishment who were appalled by her views. Her disdain for suffrage remains especially controversial, and in one way or another remains a topic of conversation in leftist circles:

> The poor, stupid, free American citizen! Free to starve, free to tramp the highways of this great country, he enjoys universal suffrage, and, by that right, he has forged chains about his limbs. The reward that he receives is stringent labor laws prohibiting the right of boycott, of picketing, in fact, of everything, except the right to be robbed of the fruits of his labor.

Her thoughts on motherhood, women's right to vote, and free love, among others, contained something to offend almost every viewpoint. Her unwavering belief in our fundamental right to joy is still so astonishingly radical in our puritan-haunted world that it feels transgressive even today. She remains a live wire in the stodgy recesses of a bookstore's philosophy section, lurking amongst the volumes waiting to beguile, seduce, and rile the unwary reader.

We've come to expect stiffness and starchiness and rigor from our philosophers, but Emma Goldman was more of a poet—wild, variable, boundlessly alive. Her views shifted and changed and evolved; she was unafraid to stand against every tide, undaunted by contradictions. It's this vital, animated quality and the flexibility of her thoughts that give her words such enduring power and the ability to speak straight to the human heart.

And to truly every human heart. How many other radical thinkers have remained so embraced by generations of American dreamers? For instance, you might be saying and who are you, without a degree in Emma Goldman Studies or even Leftist Movements or Women Anarchists or anything? And that's the point, that's the beauty of her work. She was for everyone. Not experts, not armchair revolutionaries, but us, the ordinary workers of America.

Her words can still give us guidance and inspiration. I've quoted Goldman in staff meetings and at parties and once, in a deliriously gleeful moment, in an argument with the head of one of the most prominent pro-life groups in America, a memory I will cherish and which I think Goldman would have approved of. Did she fall short in critical areas? Absolutely. Do some of her arguments not quite stand up to scrutiny? Also true. I argue that this quality actually makes her more accessible and her words of deeper usefulness. Who amongst us couldn't stand to do better, to learn more, to think more widely or think more critically? Her words, which feel more and more relevant every day now, give us a foundation to build on. Her words weren't perfect. She didn't let that stop her. Our words are not perfect. We don't have to let that stop us either.

Marriage

First published in *Firebrand*, 1897

MARRIAGE. How much sorrow, misery, humiliation; how many tears and curses; what agony and suffering has this word brought to humanity. From its very birth, up to our present day, men and women grown under the iron yoke of our marriage institution, and there seems to be no relief, no way out of it. At all times, and in all ages, have the suppressed striven to break the chains of mental and physical slavery. After thousands of noble lives have been sacrificed at the stake and on the gallows, and others have perished in prisons, or at the merciless hands of inquisitions, have the ideas of those brave heroes been accomplished. Thus have religious dogmas, feudalism and black slavery been abolished, and new ideas, more progressive, broader and clearer, have come to the front, and again we see poor down trodden humanity fighting for its rights and independence. But the crudest, most tyrannical of all institutions—marriage, stands firm as ever, and woe unto those who dare to even doubt its sacredness. Its mere discussion is enough to infuriate not only Christians and conservatives alone, but even Liberals,

Freethinkers, and Radicals. What is it that causes all these people to uphold marriage? What makes them cling to this prejudice? (for it is nothing else but prejudice). It is because marriage relations, are the foundation of private property, ergo, the foundation of our cruel and inhuman system. With wealth and superfluity on one side, crime on the other, hence to abolish marriage, means to abolish everything above mentioned. Some progressive people are trying to reform and better our marriage laws. They no longer permit the church to interfere in their matrimonial relations, others even go further, they marry free, that is without the consent of the law, but, nevertheless, this form of marriage is just as binding, just as "sacred", as the old form, because it is not the form or the kind of marriage relation we have, but the thing, the thing itself that is objectionable, hurtful and degrading. It always gives the man the right and power over his wife, not only over her body, but also over her actions, her wishes; in fact, over her whole life. And how can it be otherwise? Behind the relations of any individual man and woman to each other, stands the historical age evolved relations between the two sexes in general, which have led up to the difference in the position and privileges of the two sexes today. Two young people come together, but their relation is largely determined by causes over which they have no control. They know little of each other, society has kept both sexes apart, the boy and the girl have been brought up along different lines. Like Olive Schreiner says in her Story of an African Farm "The boy has been taught to be, the girl to seem." Exactly; the boy is taught to be intelligent, bright, clever, strong, athletic, independent and self-reliant; to develop his natural faculties, to follow his passions and desires. The girl has been taught to dress, to stand before the looking glass and admire herself, to control her emotions, her passions, her wishes, to hide her mental defects and to combine what little intelligence and ability she has on one point, and that is, the quickest and best way to angle a husband, to get profitably married. And so it has come that the two sexes hardly understand each others nature, that their mental interest and occupations are different. Public opinion separates their rights and duties, their honor and dishonor very strictly from each other. The subject of sex is a sealed book to the girl, because she has been given to understand that it is impure, immoral and indecent to even mention the sex question. To the boy it is a book whose pages have brought him disease and secret vise, and in some cases ruin and death. Among the rich class it has long been out of fashion to fall in love. Men of society marry, after a life of debauchery and lust, to build up their ruined constitution. Others again have lost their capital, in gambling sports or business speculation, and decide that an heiress would be just the thing they need, knowing well, that the marriage tie will in no way hinder them from squandering the income of their wealthy bride. The rich girl having been brought to be practical and sensible, and having been accustomed to live, breathe, eat, smile, walk and dress only according to fashion, holds out her millions to some title, or to a man with a good social standing. She has one consolation, and that is, that society allows more freedom of action to a married woman and should she be disappointed in marriage she will be in a position to gratify her wishes otherwise. We know, the walls of boudoirs and salons are deaf and dumb, and a little pleasure within these walls is no crime.

With the men and women among the working-class, marriage is quite a different thing. Love is not so rare as among the upper class, and very often helps both to endure disappointments and sorrows in life, but even here the majority of marriages, last only for a short while, to be swallowed up in the monotany of the every day life and the struggle for existence. Here also, the workingman marries because he grows tired of a bordinghouse life, and out of a desire to build a home of his own, where he will find his comfort. His main object, therefor, is to find a girl that will make a good cook and housekeeper; one that will look out only for his happiness, for his pleasures; one that will look up to him as her lord, her master, her defender, her supporter; the only ideal worth while living for. Another man hopes that the girl he'll marry will be able to work and help to put away a few cents for rainy days, but after a few months of so called happiness he awakens to the bitter reality that his wife is soon to become a mother, that she can not work, that the expenses grow bigger, and that while he before managed to get along with the small earning allowed him by his "kind" master, this earning is not sufficient to support a family.

The girl who has spent her childhood, and part of her womanhood, in the factory, feels her strength leaving her and pictures to herself the dreadful condition of ever having to remain a shopgirl, never certain of her work, she is, therefore, compelled to lookout for a man, a good husband, which means one who can support her, and give her a good home. Both, the man and the girl, marry for the same purpose, with the only exception that the man is not expected to give up his individuality, his name, his independence, whereas, the girl has to sell herself, body and soul, for the pleasure of being someone's wife; hence they do not stand on equal terms, and where there is no equality there can be no harmony. The consequence is that shortly after the first few months, or to make all allowance possible, after the first year, both come to the conclusion that marriage is a failure.

As their conditions grow worse and worse, and with the increase of children the woman grows despondent, miserable, dissatisfied and weak. Her beauty soon leaves her, and from hard work, sleepless nights, worry about the little ones and disagreement and quarrels with her husband, she soon becomes a physical wreck and curses the moment that made her a poor man's wife. Such a dreary, miserable life is certainly not inclined to maintain love or respect for each other. The man can at least forget his misery in the company of a few friends; he can absorb himself in politics, or he can drown his misfortune in a glass of beer. The woman is chained to the house by a thousand duties; she cannot, like her husband, enjoy some recreation because she either has no means for it, or she is refused the same rights as her husband, by public opinion. She has to carry the cross with her until death, because our marriage laws know of no mercy, unless she wishes to lay bare her married life before the critical eye of Mrs. Grundy, and even then she can only break the chains which tie her to the man she hates if she takes all the blame on her own shoulders, and if she has energy enough to stand before the world disgraced for the rest of her life. How many have the courage to do that? Very few. Only now and then it comes like a flash of lightning that some woman, like the Princess De Chimay, has had pluck enough to break the conventional barriers and follow her heart's desire. But this exception is a wealthy woman, dependent upon no one. The poor woman has to consider her little ones; she is less fortunate than her rich sister, and yet the woman who remains in bondage is called respectable: never mind if her whole life is a long chain of lies, deceit and treachery, she yet dares to look down with disgust upon her sisters who have been forced by society to sell their charms and affections on the street. No matter how poor, how miserable a married woman may be, she will yet think herself above the other, whom she calls a prostitute, who is an outcast, hated and despised by everyone, even those who do not hesitate to buy her embrace, look upon the poor wretch as a necessary evil, and some goody goody people even suggest to confine this evil to one district in New York, in order to "purify" all other districts of the city. What a farce! The reformers might as well demand that all the married inhabitants of New York be driven out because they certainly do not stand morally higher than the street woman. The sole difference between her and the married woman is, that the one has sold herself into chattel slavery during life, for a home or a title, and the other one sells herself for the length of time she desires; she has the right to choose the man she bestows her affections upon, whereas the married woman has no right whatsoever; she must submit to the embrace of her lord, no matter how loathsome this embrace may be to her, she must obey his commands; she has to bear him children, even at the cost of her own strength and health; in a word, she prostitutes herself every hour, every day of her life. I can find no other name for the horrid, humiliating and degrading condition of my married sisters than prostitution of the worst kind, with the only exception that the one is legal, the other illegal.

I cannot deal with the few exceptional cases of marriage which are based on love, esteem and respect; these exceptions only verify the rule. But whether legal or illegal, prostitution in any form is unnatural, hurtful and despicable, and I know only too well that the conditions cannot be changed until this infernal system is abolished, but I also know that it is not only the economic dependence of women which has caused her enslavement, but also her ignorance and prejudice, and I also know that many of my sisters could be made free even now, were it not for our marriage institutions which keep them in ignorance, stupidity and prejudice. I therefore consider it my greatest duty to denounce marriage, not only the old form, but the so-called modern marriage, the idea of taking a wife and housekeeper, the idea of private possession of one sex by the other. I demand the independence of woman; her right to support herself; to live for herself; to love whomever she pleases, or as many as she pleases. I demand freedom for both sexes, freedom of action, freedom in love and freedom in motherhood.

Do not tell me that all this can only be accomplished under Anarchy; this is entirely wrong. If we want to accomplish Anarchy, we must first have free women at least, those woman who are economically just as independent as their brothers are, and unless we have free women, we cannot have free mothers, and if mothers are not free, we cannot expect the young generation to assist us in the accomplishment of our aim, that is the establishment of an Anarchist society.

To you Freethinkers and Liberals who have abolished one God and created many whom you worship; you Radicals and Socialists, who still send your children to Sunday school, and all those who make concessions to the moral standard of to day; to all of you I say that it is your lack of courage which makes you cling to and uphold marriage, and while you admit its absurdity in theory, you have not the energy to defy public opinion, and to live your own life practically. You prate of equality of the sexes in a future Society, but you think it a necessary evil that the woman should suffer at present. You say women are inferior and weaker, and instead of assisting them to grow stronger you help to keep them in a degraded position. You demand exclusiveness for us, but you love variety and enjoy it wherever you can get a chance.

Marriage, the curse of so many centuries, the cause of jealousy, suicide and crime, must be abolished if we wish the young generation to grow to healthy, strong and free men and women.

The Child and Its Enemies

Published in *Mother Earth*, 1916

Is the child to be considered as an individuality, or as an object to be molded according to the whims and fancies of those about it? This seems to me to be the most important question to be answered by parents and educators. And whether the child is to grow from within, whether all that craves expression will be permitted to come forth toward the light of day; or whether it is to be kneaded like dough through external forces, depends upon the proper answer to this vital question.

The longing of the best and noblest of our times makes for the strongest individualities. Every sensitive being abhors the idea of being treated as a mere machine or as a mere parrot of conventionality and respectability, the human being craves recognition of his kind.

It must be borne in mind that it is through the channel of the child that the development of the mature man must go, and that the present ideas of the educating or training of the latter in the school and the family — even the family of the liberal or radical — are such as to stifle the natural growth of the child.

Every institution of our day, the family, the State, our moral codes, sees in every strong, beautiful, uncompromising personality a deadly enemy; therefore every effort is being made to cramp human emotion and originality of thought in the individual into a straight-jacket from its earliest infancy; or to shape every human being according to one pattern; not into a well-rounded individuality, but into a patient work slave, professional automaton, tax-paying citizen, or righteous moralist. If one, nevertheless, meets with real spontaneity (which, by the way, is a rare treat,) it is not due to our method of rearing or educating the child: the personality often asserts itself, regardless of official and family barriers. Such a discovery should be celebrated as an unusual event, since the obstacles placed in the way of growth and development of character are so numerous that it must be considered a miracle if it retains its strength and beauty and survives the various attempts at crippling that which is most essential to it.

Indeed, he who has freed himself from the fetters of the thoughtlessness and stupidity of the commonplace; he who can stand without moral crutches, without the approval of public opinion—private laziness, Friedrich Nietzsche called it—may well intone a high and voluminous song of independence and freedom; he has gained the right to it through fierce and fiery battles. These battles already begin at the most delicate age.

The child shows its individual tendencies in its plays, in its questions, in its association with people and things. But it has to struggle with everlasting external interference in its world of thought and emotion. It must not express itself in harmony with its nature, with its growing personality. It must become a thing, an object. Its questions are met with narrow, conventional, ridiculous replies, mostly based on falsehoods; and, when, with large, wondering, innocent eyes, it wishes to behold the wonders of the world, those about it quickly lock the windows and doors, and keep the delicate human plant in a hothouse atmosphere, where it can neither breathe nor grow freely.

Zola, in his novel "Fecundity," maintains that large sections of people have declared death to the child, have conspired against the birth of the child,—a very horrible picture indeed, yet the conspiracy entered into by civilization against the growth and making of character seems to me far more terrible and disastrous, because of the slow and gradual destruction of its latent qualities and traits and the stupefying and crippling effect thereof upon its social well-being.

Since every effort in our educational life seems to be directed toward making of the child a being foreign to itself, it must of necessity produce individuals foreign to one another, and in everlasting antagonism with each other.

The ideal of the average pedagogist is not a complete, well-rounded, original being; rather does he seek that the result of his art of pedagogy shall be automatons of flesh and blood, to best fit into the treadmill of society and the emptiness and dullness of our lives. Every home, school, college and university stands for dry, cold utilitarianism, overflooding the brain of the pupil with a tremendous amount of ideas, handed down from generations past. "Facts and data," as they are called, constitute a lot of information, well enough perhaps to maintain every form of authority and to create much awe for the importance of possession, but only a great handicap to a true understanding of the human soul and its place in the world.

Truths dead and forgotten long ago, conceptions of the world and its people, covered with mold, even during the times of our grandmothers, are being hammered into the heads of our young generation. Eternal change, thousandfold variations, continual innovation are the essence of life. Professional pedagogy knows nothing of it, the systems of education are being arranged into files, classified and numbered. They lack the strong fertile seed which, falling on rich soil, enables them to grow to great heights, they are worn and incapable of awakening spontaneity of character. Instructors and teachers, with dead souls, operate with dead values. Quantity is forced to take the place of quality. The consequences thereof are inevitable.

In whatever direction one turns, eagerly searching for human beings who do not measure ideas and emotions with the yardstick of expediency, one is confronted with the products, the herd-like drilling instead of the result of spontaneous and innate characteristics working themselves out in freedom.

> "No traces now I see
> Whatever of a spirit's agency.
> 'Tis drilling, nothing more."

These words of *Faust* fit our methods of pedagogy perfectly. Take, for instance, the way history is being taught in our schools. See how the events of the world become like a cheap puppet show, where a few wire-pullers are supposed to have directed the course of development of the entire human race.

And the history of *our own* nation! Was it not chosen by Providence to become the leading nation on earth? And does it not tower mountain high over other nations? Is it not the gem of the ocean? Is it not incomparably virtuous, ideal and brave? The result of such ridiculous teaching is a dull, shallow patriotism, blind to its own limitations, with bull-like stubbornness, utterly incapable of judging of the capacities of other nations. This is the way the spirit of youth is emasculated, deadened through an over-estimation of one's own value. No wonder public opinion can be so easily manufactured.

"Predigested food" should be inscribed over every hall of learning as a warning to all who do not wish to lose their own personalities and their original sense of judgment, who, instead, would be content with a large amount of empty and shallow shells. This may suffice as a recognition of the manifold hindrances placed in the way of an independent mental development of the child.

Equally numerous, and not less important, are the difficulties that confront the emotional life of the young. Must not one suppose that parents should be united to children by the most tender and delicate chords? One should suppose it; yet, sad as it may be, it is, nevertheless, true, that parents are the first to destroy the inner riches of their children.

The Scriptures tell us that God created Man in His own image, which has by no means proven a success. Parents follow the bad example of their heavenly master; they use every effort to shape and mold the child according to their image. They tenaciously cling to the idea that the child is merely part of themselves—an idea as false as it is injurious, and which only increases the misunderstanding of the soul of the child, of the necessary consequences of enslavement and subordination thereof.

As soon as the first rays of consciousness illuminate the mind and heart of the child, it instinctively begins to compare its own personality with the personality of those about it. How many hard and cold stone cliffs meet its large wondering gaze? Soon enough it is confronted with the painful reality that it is here only to serve as inanimate matter for parents and guardians, whose authority alone gives it shape and form.

The terrible struggle of the thinking man and woman against political, social and moral conventions owes its origin to the family, where the child is ever compelled to battle against the internal and external use of force. The categorical imperatives: You shall! you must! this is right! that is wrong! this is true! that is false! shower like a violent rain upon the unsophisticated head of the young being and impress upon its sensibilities that it has to bow before the long established and hard notions of thoughts and emotions. Yet the latent qualities and instincts seek to assert their own peculiar methods of seeking the foundation of things, of distinguishing between what is commonly called wrong, true or false. It is bent upon going its own way, since it is composed of the same nerves, muscles and blood, even as those who assume to direct its destiny. I fail to understand how parents hope that their children will ever grow up into independent, self-reliant spirits, when they strain every effort to abridge and curtail the various activities of their children, the plus in quality and character, which differentiates their offspring from themselves, and by the virtue of which they are eminently equipped carriers of new, invigorating ideas. A young delicate tree, that is being clipped and cut by the gardener in order to give it an artificial form, will never reach the majestic height and the beauty as when allowed to grow in nature and freedom.

When the child reaches adolescence, it meets, added to the home and school restrictions, with a vast amount of hard traditions of social morality. The cravings of love and sex are met with absolute ignorance by the majority of parents, who consider it as something indecent and improper, something disgraceful, almost criminal, to be suppressed and fought like some terrible disease. The love and tender feelings in the young plant are turned into vulgarity and coarseness through the stupidity of those surrounding it, so that everything fine and beautiful is either crushed altogether or hidden in the innermost depths, as a great sin, that dares not face the light.

What is more astonishing is the fact that parents will strip themselves of everything, will sacrifice everything for the physical well-being of their child, will wake nights and stand in fear and agony before some physical ailment of their beloved one; but will remain cold and indifferent, without the slightest understanding before the soul cravings and the yearnings of their child, neither hearing nor wishing to hear the loud knocking of the young spirit that demands recognition. On the contrary, they will stifle the beautiful voice of spring, of a new life of beauty and splendor of love; they will put the long lean finger of authority upon the tender throat and not allow vent to the silvery song of the individual growth, of the beauty of character, of the strength of love and human relation, which alone make life worth living.

And yet these parents imagine that they mean best for the child, and for aught I know, some really do; but their best means absolute death and decay to the bud in the making. After all, they are but imitating their own masters in State, commercial, social and moral affairs, by forcibly suppressing every independent attempt to analyze the ills of society and every sincere effort toward the abolition of these ills; never able to grasp the eternal truth that every method they employ serves as the greatest impetus to bring forth a greater longing for freedom and a deeper zeal to fight for it.

That compulsion is bound to awaken resistance, every parent and teacher ought to know. Great surprise is being expressed over the fact that the majority of children of radical parents are either altogether opposed to the ideas of the latter, many of them moving along the old antiquated paths, or that they are indifferent to the new thoughts and teachings of social regeneration. And yet there is nothing unusual in that. Radical parents, though emancipated from the belief of ownership in the human soul, still cling tenaciously to the notion that they own the child, and that they have the right to exercise their authority over it. So they set out to mold and form the child according to their own conception of what is right and wrong, forcing their ideas upon it with the same vehemence that the average Catholic parent uses. And, with the latter, they hold out the necessity before the young "to do as I tell you and not as I do." But the impressionable mind of the child realizes early enough that the lives of their parents are in contradiction to the ideas they represent; that, like the good Christian who fervently prays on Sunday, yet continues to break the Lord's commands the rest of the week, the radical parent arraigns God, priesthood, church, government, domestic authority, yet continues to adjust himself to the condition he abhors. Just so, the Freethought parent can proudly boast that his son of four will recognize the picture of Thomas Paine or Ingersoll, or that he knows that the idea of God is stupid. Or that the Social Democratic father can point to his little girl of six and say, "Who wrote the Capital, deary?" "Karl Marx, pa!" Or that the Anarchistic mother can make it known that her daughter's name is Louise Michel, Sophia Perovskaya, or that she can recite the revolutionary poems of Herwegh, Freiligrath, or Shelley, and that she will point out the faces of Spencer, Bakunin or Moses Harmon almost anywhere.

These are by no means exaggerations; they are sad facts that I have met with in my experience with radical parents. What are the results of such methods of biasing the mind? The following is the consequence, and not very infrequent, either. The child, being fed on one-sided, set and fixed ideas, soon grows weary of re-hashing the beliefs of its parents, and it sets out in quest of new sensations, no matter how inferior and shallow the new experience may be, the human mind cannot endure sameness and monotony. So it happens that that boy or girl, over-fed on Thomas Paine, will land in the arms of the Church, or they will vote for imperialism only to escape the drag of economic determinism and scientific socialism, or that they open a shirt-waist factory and cling to their right of accumulating property, only to find relief from the old-fashioned communism of their father. Or that the girl will marry the next best man, provided he can make a living, only to run away from the everlasting talk on variety.

Such a condition of affairs may be very painful to the parents who wish their children to follow in their path, yet I look upon them as very refreshing and encouraging psychological forces. They are the greatest guarantee that the independent mind, at least, will always resist every external and foreign force exercised over the human heart and head.

Some will ask, what about weak natures, must they not be protected? Yes, but to be able to do that, it will be necessary to realize that education of children is not synonymous with herdlike drilling and training. If education should really mean anything at all, it must insist upon the free growth and development of the innate forces and tendencies of the child. In this way alone can we hope for the free individual and eventually also for a free community, which shall make interference and coercion of human growth impossible.

The Social Aspects of Birth Control

Published in *Mother Earth*, April, 1916

It has been suggested that to create one genius nature uses all of her resources and takes a hundred years for her difficult task. If that be true, it takes nature even longer to create a great idea. After all, in creating a genius nature concentrates on one personality whereas an idea must eventually become the heritage of the race and must needs be more difficult to mold.

It is just one hundred and fifty years ago when a great man conceived a great idea, Robert Thomas Malthus, the father of Birth Control. That it should have taken so long a time for the human race to realize the greatness of that idea, is only one more proof of the sluggishness of the human mind. It is not possible to go into a detailed discussion of the merits of Malthus' contention, to wit, that the earth is not fertile or rich enough to supply the needs of an excessive race. Certainly if we will look across to the trenches and battlefields of Europe we will find that in a measure his premise was correct. But I feel confident that if Malthus would live to-day he would agree with all social students and revolutionists that if the masses of people continue to be poor and the rich grow ever richer, it is not because the earth is lacking in fertility and richness to supply the need even of an excessive race, but because the earth is monopolized in the hands of the few to the exclusion of the many.

Capitalism, which was in its baby's shoes during Malthus' time has since grown into a huge insatiable monster. It roars through its whistle and machine, "Send your children on to me, I will twist their bones; I will sap their blood, I will rob them of their bloom," for capitalism has an insatiable appetite.

And through its destructive machinery, militarism, capitalism proclaims, "Send your sons on to me, I will drill and discipline them until all humanity has been ground out of them; until they become automatons ready to shoot and kill at the behest of their masters." Capitalism cannot do without militarism and since the masses of people furnish the material to be destroyed in the trenches and on the battlefield, capitalism must have a large race.

In so-called good times, capitalism swallows masses of people to throw them out again in times of "industrial depression." This superfluous human mass, which is swelling the ranks of the unemployed and which represents the greatest menace in modern times, is called by our bourgeois political economists the labor margin. They will have it that under no circumstances must the labor margin diminish, else the sacred institution known as capitalistic civilization will be undermined. And so the political economists, together with all sponsors of the capitalistic regime, are in favor of a large and excessive race and are therefore opposed to Birth Control.

Nevertheless Malthus' theory contains much more truth than fiction. In its modern aspect it rests no longer upon speculation, but on other factors which are related to and interwoven with the tremendous social changes going on everywhere.

First, there is the scientific aspect, the contention on the part of the most eminent men of science who tell us that an overworked and underfed vitality cannot reproduce healthy progeny. Beside the contention of scientists, we are confronted with the terrible fact which is now even recognized by benighted people, namely, that an indiscriminate and incessant breeding on the part of the over-worked and underfed masses has resulted in an increase of defective, crippled and unfortunate children. So alarming is this fact, that it has awakened social reformers to the necessity of a mental clearing house where the cause and effect of the increase of crippled, deaf, dumb and blind children may be ascertained. Knowing as we do that reformers accept the truth when it has become apparent to the dullest in society, there need be no discussion any longer in regard to the results of indiscriminate breeding.

Secondly, there is the mental awakening of woman, that plays no small part in behalf of Birth Control. For ages she has carried her burdens. Has done her duty a thousand fold more than the soldier on the battlefield. After all, the soldier's business is to take life. For that he is paid by the State, eulogized by political charlatans and upheld by public hysteria. But woman's function is to give life, yet neither the state nor politicians nor public opinion have ever made the slightest provision in return for the life woman has given.

For ages she has been on her knees before the altar of duty as imposed by God, by Capitalism, by the State, and by Morality. To-day she has awakened from her age-long sleep. She has shaken herself free from the nightmare of the past; she has turned her face towards the light and its proclaiming in a clarion voice that she will no longer be a party to the crime of bringing hapless children into the world only to be ground into dust by the wheel of capitalism and to be torn into shreds in trenches and battlefields. And who is to say her nay? After all it is woman who is risking her health and sacrificing her youth in the reproduction of the race. Surely she ought to be in a position to decide how many children she should bring into the world, whether they should be brought into the world by the man she loves and because she wants the child, or should be born in hatred and loathing.

Furthermore, it is conceded by earnest physicians that constant reproduction on the part of women has resulted in what the laity terms, "female troubles": a lucrative condition for unscrupulous medical men. But what possible reason has woman to exhaust her system in ever-lasting child bearing?

It is precisely for this reason that women should have the knowledge that would enable her to recuperate during a period of from three to five years between each pregnancy, which alone would give her physical and mental well-being and the opportunity to take better care of the children already in existence.

But it is not woman alone who is beginning to realize the importance of Birth Control. Men, too, especially working men, have learned to see in large families a millstone around their necks, deliberately imposed upon them by the reactionary forces in society because a large family paralyzes the brain and benumbs the muscles of the masses of working men. Nothing so binds the workers to the block as a brood of children and that is exactly what the opponents of Birth Control want. Wretched as the earnings of a man with a large family are, he cannot risk even that little, so he continues in the rut, compromises and cringes before his master, just to earn barely enough to feed the many little mouths. He dare not join a revolutionary organization; he dare not go on strike; he dare not express an opinion. Masses of workers have awakened to the necessity of Birth Control as a means of freeing themselves from the terrible yoke and still more as a means of being able to do something for those already in existence by preventing more children from coming into the world.

Last, but not least, a change in the relation of the sexes, though not embracing very large numbers of people, is still making itself felt among a very considerable minority. In the past and to a large extent with the average man to-day. woman continues to be a mere object, a means to an end; largely a physical means and end. But there are men who want more than that from woman; who have come to realize that if every male were emancipated from the superstitions of the past nothing would yet be changed in the social structure so long as woman had not taken her place with him in the great social struggle. Slowly but surely these men have learned that if a woman wastes her substance in eternal pregnancies, confinements and diaper washing, she has little time left for anything else. Least of all has she time for the questions which absorb and stir the father of her children. Out of physical exhaustion and nervous stress she becomes the obstacle in the man's way and often his bitterest enemy. It is then for his own protection and also for his need of the companion and friend in the woman he loves that a great many men want her to be relieved from the terrible imposition of constant reproduction of life, that therefore they are in favor of Birth Control.

From whatever angle, then, the question of Birth Control may be considered, it is the most dominant issue of modern times and as such it cannot be driven back by persecution, imprisonment or a conspiracy of silence.

Those who oppose the Birth Control Movement claim to do so in behalf of motherhood. All the political charlatans prate about this wonderful motherhood, yet on closer examination we find that this motherhood has gone on for centuries past blindly and stupidly dedicating its offspring to Moloch. Besides, so long as mothers are compelled to work many hard hours in order to help support the creatures which they unwillingly brought into the world, the talk of motherhood is nothing else but cant. Ten percent of married women in the city of New York have to help make a living. Most of them earn the very lucrative salary of $280 a year. How dare anyone speak of the beauties of Motherhood in the face of such a crime?

But even the better paid mothers, what of them? Not so long ago our old and hoary Board of Education declared that mother teachers may not continue to teach. Though these antiquated gentlemen were compelled by public opinion to reconsider their decision, it is absolutely certain that if the average teacher were to become a mother every year, she would soon lose her position. This is the lot of the married mother; what about the unmarried mother? Or is anyone in doubt that there are thousands of unmarried mothers? They crowd our shops and factories and industries everywhere, not by choice but by economic necessity. In their drab and monotonous existence the only color left is probably a sexual attraction which without methods of prevention invariably leads to abortions. Thousands of women are sacrificed as a result of abortions because they are undertaken by quack doctors, ignorant midwives in secrecy and in haste. Yet the poets and the politicians sing of motherhood. A greater crime was never perpetrated upon woman.

Our moralists know about it, yet they persist in behalf of an indiscriminate breeding of children. They tell us that to limit offspring is entirely a modern tendency because the modern woman is loose in her morals and wishes to shirk responsibility. In reply to this, it is necessary to point out that the tendency to limit offspring is as old as the race. We have as the authority for this contention an eminent German physician Dr. Theilhaber who has compiled historic data to prove that the tendency was prevalent among the Hebrews, the Egyptians, the Persians and many tribes of American Indians. The fear of the child was so great that the women used the most hideous methods rather than to bring an unwanted child into the world. Dr. Theilhaber enumerates fifty-seven methods. This data is of great importance in as much as it dispels the superstition that woman wants to become a mother of a large family.

No, it is not because woman is lacking in responsibility, but because she has too much of the latter that she demands to know how to prevent conception. Never in the history of the world has woman been so race conscious as she is to-day. Never before has she been able to see in the child, not only in her child, but every child, the unit of society, the channel through which man and woman must pass; the strongest factor in the building of a new world. It is for this reason that Birth Control rests upon such solid ground.

We are told that so long as the law on the statute books makes the discussion of preventives a crime, these preventives must not be discussed. In reply I wish to say that it is not the Birth Control Movement, but the law, which will have to go. After all, that is what laws are for, to be made and unmade. How dare they demand that life shall submit to them? Just because some ignorant bigot in his own limitation of mind and heart succeeded in passing a law at the time when men and women were in the thralls of religious and moral superstition, must we be bound by it for the rest of our lives? I readily understand why judges and jailers shall be bound by it. It means their livelihood; their function in society. But even judges sometimes progress. I call your attention to the decision given in behalf of the issue of Birth Control by Judge Gatens of Portland, Oregon. "It seems to me that the trouble with our people today is, that there is too much prudery. Ignorance and prudery have always been the millstones around the neck of progress. We all know that things are wrong in society; that we are suffering from many evils but we have not the nerve to get up and admit it, and when some person brings to our attention something we already know, we feign modesty and feel outraged." That certainly is the trouble with most of our law makers and with all those who are opposed to Birth Control.

I am to be tried at Special Sessions April 5th. I do not know what the outcome will be, and furthermore, I do not care. This dread of going to prison for one's ideas so prevalent among American radicals, is what makes the movement so pale and weak. I have no such dread. My revolutionary tradition is that those who are not willing to go to prison for their ideas have never been considered of much value to their ideas. Besides, there are worse places than prison. But whether I have to pay for my Birth Control activities or come out free, one thing is certain, the Birth Control movement cannot be stopped nor will I be stopped from carrying on Birth Control agitation. If I refrain from discussing methods, it is not because I am afraid of a second arrest, but because for the first time in the history of America, the issue of Birth Control through oral information is clear-cut and as I want it fought out on its merits, I do not wish to give the authorities an opportunity to obscure it by something else. However, I do want to point out the utter stupidity of the law. I have at hand the testimony given by the detectives, which, according to their statement, is an exact transcription of what I spelled for them from the platform. Yet so ignorant are these men that they have not a single contracept spelled correctly now. It is perfectly within the law for the detectives to give testimony, but it is not within the law for me to read the testimony which resulted in my indictment. Can you blame me if I am an anarchist and have no use for laws? Also, I wish to point out the utter stupidity of the American court. Supposedly justice is to be meted out there. Supposedly there are to be no star chamber proceedings under democracy, yet the other day when the detectives gave their testimony, it had to be done in a whisper, close to the judge as at the confessional in a Catholic Church and under no circumstances were the ladies present permitted to hear anything that was going on. The farce of it all! And yet we are expected to respect it, to obey it, to submit to it.

I do not know how many of you are willing to do it, but I am not. I stand as one of the sponsors of a world-wide movement, a movement which aims to set woman free from the terrible yoke and bondage of enforced pregnancy; a movement which demands the right for every child to be well born; a movement which shall help free labor from its eternal dependence; a movement which shall usher into the world a new kind of motherhood. I consider this movement important and vital enough to defy all the laws upon the statute-books. I believe it will clear the way not merely for the free discussion of contracepts but for the freedom of expression in Life, Art and Labor, for the right of medical science to experiment with contracepts as it has in the treatment of tuberculosis or any other disease.

I may be arrested, I may be tried and thrown into jail, but I never will be silent; I never will acquiesce or submit to authority, nor will I make peace with a system which degrades woman to a mere incubator and which fattens on her innocent victims. I now and here declare war upon this system and shall not rest until the path has been cleared for a free motherhood and a healthy, joyous and happy childhood.

Mary Wollstonecraft, Her Tragic Life and Her Passionate Struggle for Freedom

Published in *Mother Earth*, December, 1911

THE PIONEERS of human progress are like the Seagulls, they behold new coasts, new spheres of daring thought, when their co-voyagers see only the endless stretch of water. They send joyous greetings to the distant lands. Intense, yearning, burning faith pierces the clouds of doubt, because the sharp ears of the harbingers of life discern from the maddening roar of the waves, the new message, the new symbol for humanity.

The latter does not grasp the new, dull, and inert, it meets the pioneer of truth with misgivings and resentment, as the disturber of its peace, as the annihilator of all stable habits and traditions.

Thus the pathfinders are heard only by the few, because they will not tread the beaten tracks, and the mass lacks the strength to follow into the unknown.

In conflict with every institution of their time since they will not compromise, it is inevitable that the advance guards should become aliens to the very one[s] they wish to serve; that they should be isolated, shunned, and repudiated by the nearest and dearest of kin. Yet the tragedy every pioneer must experience is not the lack of understanding — it arises from the fact that having seen new possibilities for human advancement, the pioneers can not take root in the old, and with the new still far off they become outcast roamers of the earth, restless seekers for the things they will never find.

They are consumed by the fires of compassion and sympathy for all suffering and with all their fellows, yet they are compelled to stand apart from their surroundings. Nor need they ever hope to receive the love their great souls crave, for such is the penalty of a great spirit, that what he receives is but nothing compared to what he gives.

Such was the fate and tragedy of Mary Wollstonecraft. What she gave the World, to those she loved, towered high above the average possibility to receive, nor could her burning, yearning soul content itself with the miserly crumbs that fall from the barren table of the average life.

Mary Wollstonecraft came into the World at a time when her sex was in chattel slavery: owned by the father while at home and passed on as a commodity to her husband when married. It was indeed a strange World that Mary entered into on the twenty-seventh of April

1759, yet not very much stranger than our own. For while the human race has no doubt progressed since that memorable moment, Mary Wollstonecraft is still very much the pioneer, far ahead of our own time.

She was one of many children of a middle-class family, the head of which lived up to his rights as master by tyrannizing his wife and children and squandering his capital in idle living and feasting. Who could stay him, the creator of the universe? As in many other things, so have his rights changed little, since Mary's father's time. The family soon found itself in dire want, but how were middle-class girls to earn their own living with every avenue closed to them? They had but one calling, that was marriage. Mary's sister probably realized that. She married a man she did not love in order to escape the misery of the parents' home. But Mary was made of different material, a material so finely woven it could not fit into coarse surroundings. Her intellect saw the degradation of her sex, and her soul — always at white heat against every wrong — rebelled against the slavery of half of the human race. She determined to stand on her own feet. In that determination she was strengthened by her friendship with Fannie Blood, who herself had made the first step towards emancipation by working for her own support. But even without Fannie Blood as a great spiritual force in Mary's life, nor yet even without the economic factor, she was destined by her very nature to become the Iconoclast of the false Gods whose standards the World demanded her to obey. Mary was a born rebel, one who would have created rather than submit to any form set up for her.

It has been said that nature uses a vast amount of human material to create one genius. The same holds good of the true rebel, the true pioneer. Mary was born and not made through this or that individual incident in her surroundings. The treasure of her soul, the wisdom of her life's philosophy, the depth of her World of thought, the intensity of her battle for human emancipation and especially her indomitable struggle for the liberation of her own sex, are even today so far ahead of the average grasp that we may indeed claim for her the rare exception which nature has created but once in a century. Like the Falcon who soared through space in order to behold the Sun and then paid for it with his life, Mary drained the cup of tragedy, for such is the price of wisdom.

Much has been written and said about this wonderful champion of the eighteenth century, but the subject is too vast and still very far from being exhausted. The woman's movement of today and especially the suffrage movement will find in the life and struggle of Mary Wollstonecraft much that would show them the inadequacy of mere external gain as a means of freeing their sex. No doubt much has been accomplished since Mary thundered against women's economic and political enslavement, but has that made her free? Has it added to the depth of her being? Has it brought joy and cheer in her life? Mary's own tragic life proves that economic and social rights for women alone are not enough to fill her life, nor yet enough to fill any deep life, man or woman. It is not true that the deep and fine man—I do not mean the mere male—differs very largely from the deep and fine woman. He too seeks for beauty and love, for harmony and understanding. Mary realized that, because she did not limit herself to her own sex, she demanded freedom for the whole human race.

To make herself economically independent, Mary first taught school and then accepted a position as Governess to the pampered children of a pampered lady, but she soon realized that she was unfit to be a servant and that she must turn to something that would enable her to live, yet at the same time would not drag her down. She learned the bitterness and humiliation of the economic struggle. It was not so much the lack of external comforts, that galled Mary's soul, but it was the lack of inner freedom which results from poverty and dependence which made her cry out, "How can anyone profess to be a friend to freedom yet not see that poverty is the greatest evil."

Fortunately for Mary and posterity, there existed a rare specimen of humanity, which we of the twentieth century still lack, the daring and liberal Publisher Johnson. He was the first to publish the works of Blake, of Thomas Paine, of Godwin and of all the rebels of his time without any regard to material gain. He also saw Mary's great possibilities and engaged her as proofreader, translator, and contributor to his paper, the Analytical Review. He did more. He became her most devoted friend and advisor. In fact, no other man in Mary's life was so staunch and understood her difficult nature, as did that rare man. Nor did she ever open up her soul as unreservedly to any one as she did to him. Thus she writes in one of her analytical moments:

"Life is but a jest. I am a strange compound of weakness and resolution. There is certainly a great defect in my mind, my wayward heart creates its own misery. Why I have been made thus I do not know and until I can form some idea of the whole of my existence, I must be

content to weep and dance like a child, long for a toy and be tired of it as soon as I get it. We must each of us wear a fool's cap, but mine alas has lost its bells and is grown so heavy, I find it intolerably troublesome."

That Mary should write thus of herself to Johnson shows that there must have been a beautiful comradeship between them. At any rate, thanks to her friend she found relief from the terrible struggle. She found also intellectual food. Johnson's rooms were the rendezvous of the intellectual elite of London. Thomas Paine, Godwin, Dr. Fordyce, the Painter Fuseli, and many others gathered there to discuss all the great subjects of their time.

Mary came into their sphere and became the very center of that intellectual bustle. Godwin relates how he came to hear Tom Paine at an evening arranged for him, but instead he had to listen to Mary Wollstonecraft, her conversational powers like everything else about her inevitably stood in the center of the stage.

Thus Mary could soar through space, her spirit reaching out to great heights. The opportunity soon offered itself. The erstwhile champion of English liberalism, the great Edmund Burke, delivered himself of a sentimental sermon against the French Revolution. He had met the fair Marie Antoinette and bewailed her lot at the hands of the infuriated people of Paris. His middle-class sentimentality saw in the greatest of all uprisings only the surface and not the terrible wrongs the French people endured before they were driven to their acts. But Mary Wollstonecraft saw and her reply to the mighty Burke, *The Vindication of the Rights of Man*, is one of the most powerful pleas for the oppressed and disinherited ever made.

It was written at white heat, for Mary had followed the revolution intently. Her force, her enthusiasm, and, above all, her logic and clarity of vision proved this erstwhile schoolmistress to be possessed of a tremendous brain and of a deep and passionately throbbing heart. That such should emanate from a woman was like a bomb explosion, unheard of before. It shocked the World at large, but gained for Mary the respect and affection of her male contemporaries. They felt no doubt, that she was not only their equal, but in many respects, superior to most of them.

> *"When you call yourself a friend of liberty, ask your own heart whether it would not be more consistent to style yourself the champion of Property, the adorer of the golden image which power has set up? "Security of Property! behold*

in a few words the definition of English liberty. But softly, it is only the property of the rich that is secure, the man who lives by the sweat of his brow has no asylum from oppression."

Think of the wonderful penetration in a woman more than one hundred years ago. Even today there are few among our so-called reformers, certainly very few among the women reformers, who see as clearly as this giant of the eighteenth Century. She understood only too well that mere political changes are not enough and do not strike deep into the evils of Society.

Mary Wollstonecraft on Passion:

"The regulating of passion is not always wise. On the contrary, it should seem that one reason why men have a superior judgment and more fortitude than women is undoubtedly this, that they give a freer scope to the grand passion and by more frequently going astray enlarge their minds.

"Drunkenness is due to lack of better amusement rather than to innate viciousness, crime is often the outcome of a superabundant life.

"The same energy which renders a man a daring villain would have rendered him useful to society had that society been well organized."

Mary was not only an intellectual, she was, as she says herself, possessed of a wayward heart. That is she craved love and affection. It was therefore but natural for her to be carried away by the beauty and passion of the Painter Fuseli, but whether he did not reciprocate her love, or because he lacked courage at the critical moment, Mary was forced to go through her first experience of love and pain. She certainly was not the kind of a woman to throw herself on any man's neck. Fuseli was an easy-go-lucky sort and easily carried away by Mary's beauty. But he had a wife, and the pressure of public opinion was too much for him. Be it as it may, Mary suffered keenly and fled to France to escape the charms of the artist.

Biographers are the last to understand their subject or else they would not have made so much ado of the Fuseli episode, for it was nothing else. Had the loud-mouthed Fuseli been as free as Mary to gratify their sex attraction, Mary would probably have settled down to her normal life. But he lacked courage and Mary, having been sexually starved, could not easily quench the aroused senses.

However. it required but a strong intellectual interest to bring her back to herself. And that interest she found in the stirring events of the French Revolution.

However, it was before the Fuseli incident that Mary added to her *Vindication of the Rights of Man* the *Vindication of the Rights of Woman*, a plea for the emancipation of her sex. It is not that she held man responsible for the enslavement of woman. Mary was too big and too universal to place the blame on one sex. She emphasized the fact that woman herself is a hindrance to human progress because she persists in being a sex object rather than a personality, a creative force in life. Naturally, she maintained that man has been the tyrant so long that he resents any encroachment upon his domain, but she pleaded that it was as much for his as for woman's sake that she demanded economic, political, and sexual freedom for women as the only solution to the problem of human emancipation.

> *"The laws respecting women made an absurd unit of a man and his wife and then by the easy transition of only considering him as responsible, she is reduced to a mere cypher."*

Nature has certainly been very lavish when she fashioned Mary Wollstonecraft. Not only has she endowed her with a tremendous brain, but she gave her great beauty and charm. She also gave her a deep soul, deep both in joy and sorrow. Mary was therefore doomed to become the prey of more than one infatuation. Her love for Fuseli soon made way for a more terrible, more intense love, the greatest force in her life, one that tossed her about as a willess, helpless toy in the hands of fate.

Life without love for a character like Mary is inconceivable, and it was her search and yearning for love which hurled her against the rock of inconsistency and despair.

While in Paris, Mary met in the house of T[homas] Paine where she had been welcomed as a friend, the vivacious, handsome, and elemental American, [Gilbert] Imlay. If not for Mary's love for him the World might never have known of this Gentleman. Not that he was ordinary, Mary could not have loved him with that mad passion which nearly wrecked her life. He had distinguished himself in the American War and had written a thing or two, but on the whole he would never have set the World on fire. But he set Mary on fire and held her in a trance for a considerable time.

The very force of her infatuation for him excluded harmony, but is it a matter of blame as far as Imlay is concerned? He gave her all he could, but her insatiable hunger for love could never be content with little, hence the tragedy. Then too, he was a roamer, an adventurer, an explorer into the territory of female hearts. He was possessed by the Wanderlust, could not rest at peace long anywhere. Mary needed peace, she also needed what she had never had in her family, the quiet and warmth of a home. But more than anything else she needed love, unreserved, passionate love. Imlay could give her nothing and the struggle began shortly after the mad dream had passed.

Imlay was much away from Mary at first under the pretext of business. He would not be an American to neglect his love for business. His travels brought him, as the Germans say, to other cities and other loves. As a man that was his right, equally so was it his right to deceive Mary. What she must have endured only those can appreciate who have themselves known the tempest.

All through her pregnancy with Imlay's child, Mary pined for the man, begged and called, but he was busy. The poor chap did not know that all the wealth in the world could not make up for the wealth of Mary's love. The only consolation she found was in her work. She wrote *The French Revolution* right under the very influence of that tremendous drama. Keen as she was in her observation, she saw deeper than

Burke, beneath all the terrible loss of life, she saw the still more terrible contrast between poverty and riches and [that] all the bloodshed was in vain so long as that contrast continued. Thus she wrote:

> *"If the aristocracy of birth is leveled with the ground only to make room for that of riches, I am afraid that the morale of the people will not be much improved by the change. Everything whispers to me that names not principles are changed."*

She realized while in Paris what she had predicted in her attack on Burke, that the demon of property has ever been at hand to encroach on the sacred rights of man.

With all her work Mary could not forget her love. It was after a vain and bitter struggle to bring Imlay to her that she attempted suicide. She failed, and to get back her strength she went to Norway on a mission for Imlay. She recuperated physically, but her soul was bruised and scarred. Mary and Imlay came together several times, but it was only dragging out the inevitable. Then came the final blow. Mary learned that Imlay had other affairs and that he had been deceiving her, not so much out of mischief as out of cowardice. She then took the most terrible and desperate step, she threw herself into the Thames after walking for hours to get her clothing wet [so] that she may surely drown. Oh, the inconsistencies, cry the superficial critics. But was it?

In the struggle between her intellect and her passion Mary had suffered a defeat. She was too proud and too strong to survive such a terrible blow. What else was there for her but to die?

Fate that had played so many pranks with Mary Wollstonecraft willed it otherwise. It brought her back to life and hope, only to kill her at their very doors.

She found in Godwin the first representative of Anarchist Communism, a sweet and tender camaraderie, not of the wild, primitive kind but the quiet, mature, warm sort, that soothes one like a cold hand upon a burning forehead. With him she lived consistently with her ideas in freedom, each apart from the other, sharing what they could of each other.

Again Mary was about to become a mother, not in stress and pain as the first time, but in peace and surrounded by kindness. Yet so strange is fate, that Mary had to pay with her life for the life of her little girl, Mary Godwin. She died on September tenth, 1797, barely thirty-eight years of age. Her confinement with the first child, though under the most trying of circumstances, was mere play, or as she wrote to her sister, *"an excuse for staying in bed."* Yet that tragic time demanded its victim. Fannie Imlay died of the death her mother failed to find. She committed suicide by drowning, while Mary Wollstonecraft Godwin became the wife of the sweetest lark of liberty, Shelley.

Mary Wollstonecraft, the intellectual genius, the daring fighter of the eighteenth, nineteenth, and twentieth Centuries, Mary Wollstonecraft, the woman and lover, was doomed to pain because of the very wealth of her being. With all her affairs she yet was pretty much alone, as every great soul must be alone—no doubt, that is the penalty for greatness.

Her indomitable courage in behalf of the disinherited of the earth has alienated her from her own time and created the discord in her being which alone accounts for her terrible tragedy with Imlay. Mary Wollstonecraft aimed for the highest summit of human possibilities. She was too wise and too worldly not to see the discrepancy between her world of ideals and her world of love that caused the break of the string of her delicate, complicated soul.

Perhaps it was best for her to die at that particular moment. For he who has ever tasted the madness of life can never again adjust himself to an even tenor.

But we have lost much and can only be reconciled by what she has left, and that is much. Had Mary Wollstonecraft not written a line, her life would have furnished food for thought. But she has given both, she therefore stands among the world's greatest, a life so deep, so rich, so exquisitely beautiful in her complete humanity.

Traffic in Women

Published in *Anarchism and Other Essays*, 1911

OUR REFORMERS have suddenly made a great discovery—the white slave traffic. The papers are full of these "unheard of conditions," and lawmakers are already planning a new set of laws to check the horror.

It is significant that whenever the public mind is to be diverted from a great social wrong, a crusade is inaugurated against indecency, gambling, saloons, etc. And what is the result of such crusades? Gambling is increasing, saloons are doing a lively business through back entrances, prostitution is at its height, and the system of pimps and cadets is but aggravated.

How is it that an institution, known almost to every child, should have been discovered so suddenly? How is it that this evil, known to all sociologists, should now be made such an important issue?

To assume that the recent investigation of the white slave traffic (and, by the way, a very superficial investigation) has discovered anything new, is, to say the least, very foolish. Prostitution has been, and is, a widespread evil, yet mankind goes on its business, perfectly indifferent to the sufferings and distress of the victims of prostitution. As indifferent, indeed, as mankind has remained to our industrial system, or to economic prostitution.

Only when human sorrows are turned into a toy with glaring colors will baby people become interested—for a while at least. The people are a very fickle baby that must have new toys every day. The "righteous" cry against the white slave traffic is such a toy. It serves to amuse the people for a little while, and it will help to create a few more fat political jobs—parasites who stalk about the world as inspectors, investigators, detectives, and so forth. What is really the cause of the trade in women? Not merely white women, but yellow and black women as well. Exploitation, of course; the merciless Moloch of capitalism that fattens on underpaid labor, thus driving thousands of women and girls into prostitution. With Mrs. Warren, these girls feel, "Why waste your life working for a few shillings a week in a scullery, eighteen hours a day?"

Naturally our reformers say nothing about this cause. They know it well enough, but it doesn't pay to say anything about it. It is much more profitable to play the Pharisee, to pretend an outraged morality, than to go to the bottom of things.

However, there is one commendable exception among the young writers: Reginald Wright Kauffman, whose work, *The House of Bondage*, is the first earnest attempt to treat the social evil, not from a sentimental Philistine viewpoint. A journalist of wide experience, Mr. Kauffman proves that our industrial system leaves most women no alternative except prostitution. The women portrayed in *The House of Bondage* belong to the working class. Had the author portrayed the life of women in other spheres, he would have been confronted with the same state of affairs.

Nowhere is woman treated according to the merit of her work, but rather as a sex. It is therefore almost inevitable that she should pay for her right to exist, to keep a position in whatever line, with sex favors. Thus it is merely a question of degree whether she sells herself to one man, in or out of marriage, or to many men. Whether our reformers admit it or not, the economic and social inferiority of woman is responsible for prostitution.

Just at present our good people are shocked by the disclosures that in New York City alone, one out of every ten women works in a factory, that the average wage received by women is six dollars per week for forty-eight to sixty hours of work, and that the majority of female wage workers face many months of idleness which leaves the average wage about $280 a year. In view of these economic horrors, is it to be wondered at that prostitution and the white slave trade have become such dominant factors?

Lest the preceding figures be considered an exaggeration, it is well to examine what some authorities on prostitution have to say:

"A prolific cause of female depravity can be found in the several tables, showing the description of the employment pursued, and the wages received, by the women previous to their fall, and it will be a question for the political economist to decide how far mere business consideration should be an apology on the part of employers for a reduction in their rates of remuneration, and whether the savings of a small percentage on wages is not more than counter-balanced by the enormous amount of taxation enforced on the public at large to defray the expenses incurred on account of a system of vice, *which is the direct result, in many cases, of insufficient compensation of honest labor.*"*

---

* Dr. Sanger, *The History Of Prostitution*

Our present-day reformers would do well to look into Dr. Sanger's book. There, they will find that out of 2,000 cases under his observation, but few came from the middle classes, from well-ordered conditions, or pleasant homes. By far the largest majority were working girls and working women; some driven into prostitution through sheer want, others because of a cruel, wretched life at home, others again because of thwarted and crippled physical natures (of which I shall speak later on). Also it will do the maintainers of purity and morality good to learn that out of two thousand cases, 490 were married women, women who lived with their husbands. Evidently there was not much of a guarantee for their "safety and purity" in the sanctity of marriage.*

Dr. Alfred Blaschko, in *Prostitution in the Nineteenth Century*, is even more emphatic in characterizing economic conditions as one of the most vital factors of prostitution.

"Although prostitution has existed in all ages, it was left to the nineteenth century to develop it into

---

* It is a significant fact that Dr. Sanger's book has been excluded from the U.S. mails. Evidently the authorities are not anxious that the public be informed as to the true cause of prostitution.

a gigantic social institution. The development of industry with vast masses of people in the competitive market, the growth and congestion of large cities, the insecurity and uncertainty of employment, has given prostitution an impetus never dreamed of at any period in human history."

And again Havelock Ellis, while not so absolute in dealing with the economic cause, is nevertheless compelled to admit that it is indirectly and directly the main cause. Thus he finds that a large percentage of prostitutes is recruited from the servant class, although the latter have less care and greater security. On the other hand, Mr. Ellis does not deny that the daily routine, the drudgery, the monotony of the servant girl's lot, and especially the fact that she may never partake of the companionship and joy of a home, is no mean factor in forcing her to seek recreation and forgetfulness in the gaiety and glimmer of prostitution. In other words, the servant girl, being treated as a drudge, never having the right to herself and worn out by the caprices of her mistress, can find an outlet, like the factory or shopgirl, only in prostitution.

The most amusing side of the question now before the public is the indignation of our "good, respectable people," especially the various Christian gentlemen, who are always to be found in the front ranks of every crusade. Is it that they are absolutely ignorant of the history of religion, and especially of the Christian religion? Or is it that they hope to blind the present generation to the part played in the past by the Church in relation to prostitution? Whatever their reason, they should be the last to cry out against the unfortunate victims of today, since it is known to every intelligent student that prostitution is of religious origin, maintained and fostered for many centuries, not as a shame but as a virtue, hailed as such by the Gods themselves.

"It would seem that the origin of prostitution is to be found primarily in a religious custom, religion, the great conserver of social tradition, preserving in a transformed shape a primitive freedom that was passing out of the general social life. The typical example is that recorded by Herodotus, in the fifth century before Christ, at the Temple of Mylitta, the Babylonian Venus, where every woman, once in her life, had to come and give herself to the first stranger, who threw a coin in her lap, to worship the goddess. Very similar customs existed in other parts of Western Asia, in North Africa, in Cyprus, and other islands of the Eastern Mediterranean, and also in Greece, where the temple of Aphrodite on the fort at Corinth possessed over a thousand hierodules, dedicated to the service of the goddess.

"The theory that religious prostitution developed, as a general rule, out of the belief that the generative activity of human beings possessed a mysterious and sacred influence in promoting the fertility of Nature, is maintained by all authoritative writers on the subject. Gradually, however, and when prostitution became an organized institution under priestly influence, religious prostitution developed utilitarian sides, thus helping to increase public revenue.

"The rise of Christianity to political power produced little change in policy. The leading fathers of the Church tolerated prostitution. Brothels under municipal protection are found in the thirteenth century. They constituted a sort of public service, the directors of them being considered almost as public servants."*

To this must be added the following from Dr. Sanger's work:

"Pope Clement II. issued a bull that prostitutes would be tolerated if they pay a certain amount of their earnings to the Church.

---

* Havelock Ellis, *Sex and Society*

"Pope Sixtus IV. was more practical; from one single brothel, which he himself had built, he received an income of 20,000 ducats."

In modern times the Church is a little more careful in that direction. At least she does not openly demand tribute from prostitutes. She finds it much more profitable to go in for real estate, like Trinity Church, for instance, to rent out death traps at an exorbitant price to those who live off and by prostitution.

Much as I should like to, my space will not admit speaking of prostitution in Egypt, Greece, Rome, and during the Middle Ages. The conditions in the latter period are particularly interesting, inasmuch as prostitution was organized into guilds, presided over by a brothel Queen. These guilds employed strikes as a medium of improving their condition and keeping a standard price. Certainly that is more practical a method than the one used by the modern wage slave in society.

It would be one-sided and extremely superficial to maintain that the economic factor is the only cause of prostitution. There are others no less important and vital. That, too, our reformers know, but dare discuss even less than the institution that saps the very life out of both men and women. I refer to the sex question, the very mention of which causes most people moral spasms.

It is a conceded fact that woman is being reared as a sex commodity, and yet she is kept in absolute ignorance of the meaning and importance of sex. Everything dealing with the subject is suppressed, and persons who attempt to bring light into this terrible darkness are persecuted and thrown into prison. Yet it is nevertheless true that so long as a girl is not to know how to take care of herself, not to know the function of the most important part of her life, we need not be surprised if she becomes an easy prey to prostitution, or to any other form of a relationship which degrades her to the position of an object for mere sex gratification.

It is due to this ignorance that the entire life and nature of the girl is thwarted and crippled. We have long ago taken it as a self-evident fact that the boy may follow the call of the wild; that is to say, that the boy may, as soon as his sex nature asserts itself, satisfy that nature; but our moralists are scandalized at the very thought that the nature of a girl should assert itself. To the moralist, prostitution does not consist so much in the fact that the woman sells her body, but rather that she sells it out of wedlock. That this is no mere statement is proved by the fact that marriage for monetary considerations is perfectly legitimate, sanctified by law and public opinion, while any other union is condemned and repudiated. Yet a prostitute, if properly defined, means nothing else than "any person for whom sexual relationships are subordinated to gain."*

"Those women are prostitutes who sell their bodies for the exercise of the sexual act and make of this a profession."**

In fact, Banger goes further; he maintains that the act of prostitution is "intrinsically equal to that of a man or woman who contracts a marriage for economic reasons."

Of course, marriage is the goal of every girl, but as thousands of girls cannot marry, our stupid social customs condemn them either to a life of celibacy or prostitution. Human nature asserts itself regardless of all laws, nor is there any plausible reason why nature should adapt itself to a perverted conception of morality.

Society considers the sex experiences of a man as attributes of his general development, while similar experiences in the life of a woman are looked upon

---

* Guyot, *La Prostitution*

** Banger, *Criminalite et Condition Economique*

as a terrible calamity, a loss of honor and of all that is good and noble in a human being. This double standard of morality has played no little part in the creation and perpetuation of prostitution. It involves the keeping of the young in absolute ignorance on sex matters, which alleged "innocence," together with an overwrought and stifled sex nature, helps to bring about a state of affairs that our Puritans are so anxious to avoid or prevent.

Not that the gratification of sex must needs lead to prostitution; it is the cruel, heartless, criminal persecution of those who dare divert from the beaten paths, which is responsible for it.

Girls, mere children, work in crowded, over-heated rooms ten to twelve hours daily at a machine, which tends to keep them in a constant over-excited sex state. Many of these girls have no home or comforts of any kind; therefore the street or some place of cheap amusement is the only means of forgetting their daily routine. This naturally brings them into close proximity with the other sex. It is hard to say which of the two factors brings the girl's over-sexed condition to a climax, but it is certainly the most natural thing that a climax should result. That is the first step toward prostitution. Nor is the girl to be held responsible for it. On the contrary, it is altogether the fault of society, the fault of our lack of understanding, of our lack of appreciation of life in the making; especially is it the criminal fault of our moralists, who condemn a girl for all eternity, because she has gone from the "path of virtue;" that is, because her first sex experience has taken place without the sanction of the Church.

The girl feels herself a complete outcast, with the doors of home and society closed in her face. Her entire training and tradition is such that the girl herself feels depraved and fallen, and therefore has no ground to stand upon, or any hold that will lift her up, instead of dragging her down. Thus society creates the victims that it afterwards vainly attempts to get rid of. The meanest, most depraved and decrepit man still considers himself too good to take as his wife the woman whose grace he was quite willing to buy, even though he might thereby save her from a life of horror. Nor can she turn to her own sister for help. In her stupidity, the latter deems herself too pure and chaste, not realizing that her own position is in many respects even more deplorable than her sister's of the street.

"The wife who married for money, compared with the prostitute," says Havelock Ellis, "is the true scab.

She is paid less, gives much more in return in labor and care, and is absolutely bound to her master. The prostitute never signs away the right over her own person, she retains her freedom and personal rights, nor is she always compelled to submit to a man's embrace."

Nor does the better-than-thou woman realize the apologist claim of Lecky that "though she may be the supreme type of vice, she is also the most efficient guardian of virtue. But for her, happy homes would be polluted, unnatural and harmful practice would abound."

Moralists are ever ready to sacrifice one-half of the human race for the sake of some miserable institution which they can not outgrow. As a matter of fact, prostitution is no more a safeguard for the purity of the home than rigid laws are a safeguard against prostitution. Fully fifty percent of married men are patrons of brothels. It is through this virtuous element that the married women—nay, even the children— are infected with venereal diseases. Yet society has not a word of condemnation for the man, while no law is too monstrous to be set in motion against the helpless victim. She is not only preyed upon by those who use her. but she is also absolutely at the mercy of every policeman and miserable detective on the beat, the officials at the station house, the authorities in every prison.

In a recent book by a woman who was for twelve years the mistress of a "house" are to be found the following figures: "The authorities compelled me to pay every month fines between $14.70 to $29.70, the girls would pay from $5.70 to $9.70 to the police." Considering that the writer did her business in a small city, that the amounts she gives do not include extra bribes and fines, one can readily see the tremendous revenue the police department derives from the blood money of its victims, whom it will not even protect. Woe to those who refuse to pay their toll; they would be rounded up like cattle, "if only to make a favorable impression upon the good citizens of the city, or if the powers needed extra money on the side. For the warped mind who believes that a fallen woman is incapable of human emotion, it would be impossible to realize the grief, the disgrace, the tears, the wounded pride that was ours every time we were pulled in."

Strange, isn't it, that a woman who has a kept a "house" should be able to feel that way? But stranger still that a good Christian world should bleed and fleece such women, and give them nothing in return except obloquy and persecution. Oh, for the charity of a Christian world!

Much stress is laid on white slaves being imported into America. How would America ever retain her virtue if Europe did not help her out? I will not deny that this may be the case in some instances, any more than I will deny that there are emissaries of Germany and other countries luring economic slaves into America; but I absolutely deny that prostitution is recruited to any appreciable extent from Europe. It may be true that the majority of prostitutes in New York City are foreigners, but that is because the majority of the population is foreign. The moment we go to any other American city, to Chicago or the Middle West, we shall find that the number of foreign prostitutes is by far a minority.

Equally exaggerated is the belief that the majority of street girls in this city were engaged in this business before they came to America. Most of the girls speak excellent English, are Americanized in habits and appearance—a thing absolutely impossible unless they had lived in this country many years. That is, they were driven into prostitution by American conditions, by the thoroughly American custom for excessive display of finery and clothes, which, of course, necessitates money—money that cannot be earned in shops or factories.

In other words, there is no reason to believe that any set of men would go to the risk and expense of getting foreign products when American conditions are overflooding the market with thousands of girls. On the other hand, there is sufficient evidence to prove that the export of American girls for the purpose of prostitution is by no means a small factor.

Thus Clifford G. Roe, ex-Assistant State Attorney of Cook County, Ill., makes the open charge that New England girls are shipped to Panama for the express use of men in the employ of Uncle Sam. Mr. Roe adds that "there seems to be an underground railroad between Boston and Washington which many girls travel." Is it not significant that the railroad should lead to the very seat of Federal authority? That Mr. Roe said more than was desired in certain quarters is proved by the fact that he lost his position. It is not practical for men in office to tell tales from school.

The excuse given for the conditions in Panama is that there are no brothels in the Canal Zone. That is the usual avenue of escape for a hypocritical world that dares not face the truth. Not in the Canal Zone, not in the city limits—therefore prostitution does not exist.

Next to Mr. Roe, there is James Bronson Reynolds, who has made a thorough study of the white slave traffic in Asia. As a staunch American citizen and friend of the future Napoleon of America, Theodore Roosevelt, he is surely the last to discredit the virtue of his country. Yet we are informed by him that in Hong Kong, Shanghai, and Yokohama, the Augean stables of American vice are located. There, American prostitutes have made themselves so conspicuous that in the Orient, "American girl" is synonymous with prostitute. Mr. Reynolds reminds his countrymen that while Americans in China are under the protection of our consular representatives, the Chinese in America have no protection at all. Everyone who knows the brutal and barbarous persecution Chinese and Japanese endure on the Pacific Coast, will agree with Mr. Reynolds.

In view of the above facts it is rather absurd to point to Europe as the swamp whence come all the social diseases of America. Just as absurd is it to proclaim the myth that the Jews furnish the largest contingent of willing prey. I am sure that no one will accuse me of nationalistic tendencies. I am glad to say that I have developed out of them, as out of many other prejudices. If, therefore, I resent the statement that Jewish prostitutes are imported, it is not because of any Judaistic sympathies, but because of the facts inherent in the lives of these people. No one but the most superficial will claim that Jewish girls migrate to strange lands, unless they have some tie or relation that brings them there. The Jewish girl is not adventurous. Until recent years, she had never left home, not even so far as the next village or town, except it were to visit some relative. Is it then credible that Jewish girls would leave their parents or families, travel thousands of miles to strange lands, through the influence and promises of strange forces? Go to any of the large incoming steamers and see for yourself if these girls do not come either with their parents, brothers, aunts or other kinsfolk. There may be exceptions, of course, but to state that large numbers of Jewish girls are imported for prostitution, or any other purpose, is simply not to know Jewish psychology.

Those who sit in a glass house do wrong to throw stones about them; besides, the American glass house is rather thin, it will break easily, and the interior is anything but a gainly sight.

To ascribe the increase in prostitution to alleged importation, to the growth of the cadet system, or similar causes, is highly superficial. I have already referred to the former. As to the cadet system, abhorrent as it is, we must not ignore the fact that it is essentially a phase of modern prostitution—a phase accentuated by suppression and graft, resulting from sporadic crusades against the social evil.

The procurer is no doubt a poor specimen of the human family, but in what manner is he more despicable than the policeman who takes the last cent from the street walker and then locks her up in the station house? Why is the cadet more criminal, or a greater menace to society, than the owners of department stores and factories, who grow fat on the sweat of their victims, only to drive them to the streets? I make no plea for the cadet, but I fail to see why he should be mercilessly hounded, while the real perpetrators of all social iniquity enjoy immunity and respect. Then, too, it is well to remember that it is not the cadet who makes the prostitute. It is our sham and hypocrisy that create both the prostitute and the cadet.

Until 1894, very little was known in America of the procurer. Then we were attacked by an epidemic of virtue. Vice was to be abolished, the country purified at all cost. The social cancer was therefore driven out of sight, but deeper into the body. Keepers of brothels, as well as their unfortunate victims, were turned over to the tender mercies of the police. The inevitable consequence of exorbitant bribes, and the penitentiary, followed.

While comparatively protected in the brothels, where they represented a certain monetary value, the girls now found themselves on the street, absolutely at the mercy of the graft-greedy police. Desperate, needing protection and longing for affection, these girls naturally proved an easy prey for cadets, themselves the result of the spirit of our commercial age. Thus the cadet system was the direct outgrowth of police persecution, graft, and attempted suppression of prostitution. It were sheer folly to confound this modern phase of the social evil with the causes of the latter.

Mere suppression and barbaric enactments can serve but to embitter, and further degrade, the unfortunate victims of ignorance and stupidity. The latter has reached its highest expression in the proposed law to make humane treatment of prostitutes a crime, punishing any one sheltering a prostitute with five years' imprisonment and $10,000 fine. Such an attitude merely exposes the terrible lack of understanding of the true causes of prostitution, as a social factor, as well as manifesting the Puritanic spirit of the Scarlet Letter days.

There is not a single modern writer on the subject who does not refer to the utter futility of legislative methods in coping with the issue. Thus Dr. Blaschko finds that governmental suppression and moral crusades accomplish nothing save driving the evil into secret channels, multiplying its dangers to society. Havelock Ellis, the most thorough and humane student of prostitution, proves by a wealth of data that the more stringent the methods of persecution, the worse the condition becomes. Among other data, we learn that in France, "in 1560, Charles IX. abolished brothels through an edict, but the numbers of prostitutes were only increased, while many new brothels appeared in unsuspected shapes, and were more dangerous. In spite of all such legislation, *or because of it*, there has been no country in which prostitution has played a more conspicuous part."*

An educated public opinion, freed from the legal and moral hounding of the prostitute, can alone help to ameliorate present conditions. Willful shutting of eyes and ignoring of the evil as a social factor of modern life, can but aggravate matters. We must rise above our foolish

---

* *Sex and Society*

notions of "better than thou" and learn to recognize in the prostitute a product of social conditions. Such a realization will sweep away the attitude of hypocrisy, and ensure a greater understanding and more humane treatment. As to a thorough eradication of prostitution, nothing can accomplish that, save a complete transvaluation of all accepted values—especially the moral ones—coupled with the abolition of industrial slavery.

WOMEN SUFFRAGE

Published in *Anarchism and Other Essays*, 1911

We boast of the age of advancement, of science, and progress. Is it not strange, then, that we still believe in fetish worship? True, our fetiches have different form and substance, yet in their power over the human mind they are still as disastrous as were those of old.

Our modern fetich is universal suffrage. Those who have not yet achieved that goal fight bloody revolutions to obtain it, and those who have enjoyed its reign bring heavy sacrifice to the altar of this omnipotent deity. Woe to the heretic who dare question that divinity!

Woman, even more than man, is a fetish worshipper, and though her idols may change, she is ever on her knees, ever holding up her hands, ever blind to the fact that her god has feet of clay. Thus woman has been the greatest supporter of all deities from time immemorial. Thus, too, she has had to pay the price that only gods can exact—her freedom, her heart's blood, her very life.

Nietzsche's memorable maxim, "When you go to woman, take the whip along," is considered very brutal, yet Nietzsche expressed in one sentence the attitude of woman towards her gods.

Religion, especially the Christian religion, has condemned woman to the life of an inferior, a slave. It has thwarted her nature and fettered her soul, yet the Christian religion has no greater supporter, none more devout, than woman. Indeed, it is safe to say that religion would have long ceased to be a factor in the lives of the people if it were not for the support it receives from woman. The most ardent churchworkers, the most tireless missionaries the world over, are women, always sacrificing on the altar of the gods that have chained her spirit and enslaved her body.

The insatiable monster, war, robs woman of all that is dear and precious to her. It exacts her brothers, lovers, sons, and in return gives her a life of loneliness and despair. Yet the greatest supporter and worshiper of war is woman. She it is who instills the love of conquest and power into her children; she it is who whispers the glories of war into the ears of her little ones, and who rocks her baby to sleep with the tunes of trumpets and the noise of guns. It is woman, too, who crowns the victor on his return from the battlefield.

Yes, it is woman who pays the highest price to that insatiable monster, war.

Then there is the home. What a terrible fetish it is! How it saps the very life-energy of woman—this modern prison with golden bars. Its shining aspect blinds woman to the price she would have to pay as wife, mother and housekeeper. Yet woman clings tenaciously to the home, to the power that holds her in bondage.

It may be said that because woman recognizes the awful toll she is made to pay to the Church, State, and the home, she wants suffrage to set herself free. That may be true of the few; the majority of suffragists repudiate utterly such blasphemy. On the contrary, they insist always that it is woman suffrage which will make her a better Christian and homekeeper, a staunch citizen of the State. Thus suffrage is only a means of strengthening the omnipotence of the very Gods that woman has served from time immemorial.

What wonder, then, that she should be just as devout, just as zealous, just as prostrate before the new idol, woman suffrage. As of old, she endures persecution, imprisonment, torture and all forms of condemnation with a smile on her face. As of old, the most enlightened, even, hope for a miracle from the twentieth century deity—suffrage. Life, happiness, joy, freedom, independence—all that, and more, is to spring from suffrage. In her blind devotion woman does not see what people of intellect perceived fifty years ago: that suffrage is an evil, that it has only helped to enslave people, that it has but closed their eyes that they may not see how craftily they were made to submit.

Woman's demand for equal suffrage is based largely on the contention that woman must have the equal right in all affairs of society. No one could possibly refute that if suffrage were a right. Alas, for the ignorance of the human mind, which can see a right in an imposition. Or is it not the most brutal imposition for one set of people to make laws that another set is coerced by force to obey? Yet woman clamors for that "golden opportunity" that has wrought so much misery in the world, and robbed man of his integrity and self-reliance; an imposition which has thoroughly corrupted the people, and made them absolute prey in the hands of unscrupulous politicians.

The poor, stupid, free American citizen! Free to starve, free to tramp the highways of this great country, he enjoys universal suffrage, and, by that right, he has forged chains about his limbs. The reward that he receives is stringent labor laws prohibiting the right of boycott, of picketing, in fact, of everything, except the right to be robbed of the fruits of his labor. Yet all these disastrous results of the twentieth century fetish have taught woman nothing. But, then, woman will purify politics, we are assured.

Needless to say, I am not opposed to woman suffrage on the conventional ground that she is not equal to it. I see neither physical, psychological, nor mental reasons why woman should not have the equal right to vote with man. But that cannot possibly blind me to the absurd notion that woman will accomplish that wherein man has failed. If she would not make things worse, she certainly could not make them better. To assume, therefore, that she would succeed in purifying something which is not susceptible of purification is to credit her with supernatural powers. Since woman's greatest misfortune has been that she was looked upon as either angel or devil, her true salvation lies in being placed on earth; namely, in being considered human, and therefore subject to all human follies and mistakes. Are we, then, to believe that two errors will make a right? Are we to assume that the poison already inherent in politics will be decreased, if women were to enter the political arena? The most ardent suffragists would hardly maintain such a folly.

As a matter of fact, the most advanced students of universal suffrage have come to realize that all existing systems of political power are absurd and are completely inadequate to meet the pressing issues of life. This view is also borne out by a statement of one who is herself an ardent believer in woman suffrage, Dr. Helen L. Sumner. In her able work on Equal Suffrage, she says: "In Colorado, we find that equal suffrage serves to show in the most striking way the essential rottenness and degrading character of the existing system." Of course, Dr. Sumner has in mind a particular system of voting, but the same applies with equal force to the entire machinery of the representative system. With such a basis, it is difficult to understand how woman, as a political factor, would benefit either herself or the rest of mankind.

But, say our suffrage devotees, look at the countries and States where female suffrage exists. See what woman has accomplished—in Australia, New Zealand, Finland, the Scandinavian countries, and in our own four States, Idaho, Colorado, Wyoming and Utah. Distance lends enchantment—or, to quote a Polish formula—"it is well where we are not." Thus, one would assume that those countries and States are unlike other countries or States, that they have greater freedom, greater social and economic equality, a finer appreciation of human life, deeper understanding of the great social struggle, with all the vital questions it involves for the human race.

The women of Australia and New Zealand can vote and help make the laws. Are the labor conditions better there than they are in England, where the suffragettes are making such a heroic struggle? Does there exist a greater motherhood, happier and freer children than in England? Is woman there no longer considered a mere sex commodity? Has she emancipated herself from the Puritanical double standard of morality for men and women? Certainly none but the ordinary female stump politician will dare answer these questions in the affirmative. If that be so, it seems ridiculous to point to Australia and New Zealand as the Mecca of equal suffrage accomplishments.

On the other hand, it is a fact to those who know the real political conditions in Australia, that politics have gagged labor by enacting the most stringent labor laws, making strikes without the sanction of an arbitration committee a crime equal to treason.

Not for a moment do I mean to imply that woman suffrage is responsible for this state of affairs. I do mean, however, that there is no reason to point to Australia as a wonder-worker of woman's accomplishment, since her influence has been unable to free labor from the thralldom of political bossism.

Finland has given woman equal suffrage; nay, even the right to sit in Parliament. Has that helped to develop a greater heroism, an intenser zeal than that of the women of Russia? Finland, like Russia, smarts under the terrible whip of the bloody Tsar. Where are the Finnish Perovskaias, Spiridonovas, Figners, Breshkovskaias? Where are the countless numbers of Finnish young girls who cheerfully go to Siberia for their cause? Finland is sadly in need of heroic liberators. Why has the ballot not created them? The only Finnish avenger of his people was a man, not a woman, and he used a more effective weapon than the ballot.

As to our own States where women vote, and which are constantly being pointed out as examples of marvels, what has been accomplished there through the ballot that women do not to a large extent enjoy in other States or that they could not achieve through energetic efforts without the ballot? True, in the suffrage States women are guaranteed equal rights to property; but of what avail is that right to the mass of women without property, the thousands of wage workers who live from hand to mouth? That equal suffrage did not, and cannot, affect their condition is admitted even by Dr. Sumner, who certainly is in a position to know. As an ardent suffragist, and having been sent to Colorado by the Collegiate Equal Suffrage League of New York State to collect material in favor of suffrage, she would be the last to say anything derogatory; yet we are informed that "equal suffrage has but slightly affected the economic conditions of women. That women do not receive equal pay for equal work and that, though woman in Colorado has enjoyed school suffrage since 1876, women teachers are paid less than in California." On the other hand, Miss Sumner fails to account for the fact that although women have had school suffrage for thirty-four years, and equal suffrage since 1894, the census in Denver alone a few months ago disclosed the fact of fifteen thousand defective school children. And that, too, with mostly women in the educational department, and also notwithstanding that women in Colorado have passed the "most stringent laws for child and animal protection." The women of Colorado "have taken great interest in the State institutions for the care of dependent, defective and delinquent children." What a horrible indictment against woman's care and interest, if one city has fifteen thousand defective children. What about the glory of woman suffrage, since it has failed utterly in the most important social issue, the child? And where is the superior sense of justice that woman was to bring into the political field? Where was it in 1903, when the mine owners waged a guerilla war against the Western Miners' Union; when General Bell established a reign of terror, pulling men out of beds at night, kidnapping them across the border line, throwing them into bull pens, declaring "to hell with the Constitution, the club is the Constitution?" Where were the women politicians then, and why did they not exercise the power of their vote? But they did. They helped to defeat the most fair-minded and liberal man, Governor Waite. The latter had to make way for the tool of the mine kings, Governor Peabody, the enemy of labor, the Tsar of Colorado. "Certainly male suffrage could have done nothing worse." Granted. Wherein, then, are the advantages to woman and society from woman suffrage? The oft-repeated assertion that woman will purify politics is also but a myth. It is not borne out by the people who know the political conditions of Idaho, Colorado, Wyoming and Utah.

Woman, essentially a purist, is naturally bigotted and relentless in her effort to make others as good as she thinks they ought to be. Thus, in Idaho, she has disfranchised her sister of the street, and declared all women of "lewd character" unfit to vote. "Lewd" not being interpreted, of course, as prostitution *in* marriage. It goes without saying that illegal prostitution and gambling have been prohibited. In this regard, the law must needs be of feminine nature: It always prohibits. Therein all laws are wonderful. They go no further, but their very tendencies open all the floodgates of hell. Prostitution and gambling have never done a more flourishing business than since the law has been set against them.

In Colorado, the Puritanism of woman has expressed itself in a more drastic form. "Men of notoriously unclean lives, and men connected with saloons, have been dropped from politics since women have the vote."* Could brother Comstock do more? Could all the Puritan fathers have done more? I wonder how many women realize the gravity of this would-be feat. I wonder if they understand that it is the very thing which, instead of elevating woman, has made her a political spy, a contemptible pry into the private affairs of people, not so much for the good of the cause, but because, as a Colorado woman said, "they like to get into houses they have never been in, and find out all they can, politically and otherwise."**

* *Equal Suffrage*, Dr. Helen A. Sumner

** *Ibid.*

Yes, and into the human soul and its minutest nooks and corners. For nothing satisfies the craving of most women so much as scandal. And when did she ever enjoy such opportunities as are hers, the politician's?

"Notoriously unclean lives, and men connected with the saloons." Certainly, the lady vote gatherers cannot be accused of much sense of proportion. Granting even that these busybodies can decide whose lives are clean enough for that eminently clean atmosphere, politics, must it follow that saloon-keepers belong to the same category? Unless it be American hypocrisy and bigotry, so manifest in the principle of Prohibition, which sanctions the spread of drunkenness among men and women of the rich class, yet keeps vigilant watch on the only place left to the poor man. If no other reason, woman's narrow and purist attitude toward life makes her a greater danger to liberty wherever she has political power. Man has long overcome the superstitions that still engulf woman. In the economic competitive field, man has been compelled to exercise efficiency, judgment, ability, competency. He therefore had neither time nor inclination to measure everyone's morality with a Puritanic yardstick. In his political activities, too, he has not gone about blindfolded. He knows that quantity and not quality is the material for the political grinding mill, and, unless he is a sentimental reformer or an old fossil, he knows that politics can never be anything but a swamp.

Women who are at all conversant with the process of politics, know the nature of the beast, but in their self-sufficiency and egotism they make themselves believe that they have but to pet the beast, and he will become as gentle as a lamb, sweet and pure. As if women have not sold their votes, as if women politicians cannot be bought! If her body can be bought in return for material consideration, why not her vote? That it is being done in Colorado and in other States, is not denied even by those in favor of woman suffrage.

As I have said before, woman's narrow view of human affairs is not the only argument against her as a politician superior to man. There are others. Her life-long economic parasitism has utterly blurred her conception of the meaning of equality. She clamors for equal rights with men, yet we learn that "few women care to canvas in undesirable districts."* How little equality means to them compared with the Russian women, who face hell itself for their ideal!

Woman demands the same rights as man, yet she is indignant that her presence does not strike him dead:

---

* Dr. Helen A. Sumner

he smokes, keeps his hat on and does not jump from his seat like a flunkey. These may be trivial things, but they are nevertheless the key to the nature of American suffragists. To be sure, their English sisters have outgrown these silly notions. They have shown themselves equal to the greatest demands on their character and power of endurance. All honor to the heroism and sturdiness of the English suffragettes. Thanks to their energetic, aggressive methods, they have proved an inspiration to some of our own lifeless and spineless ladies. But after all, the suffragettes, too, are still lacking in appreciation of real equality. Else how is one to account for the tremendous, truly gigantic effort set in motion by those valiant fighters for a wretched little bill which will benefit a handful of propertied ladies, with absolutely no provision for the vast mass of workingwomen? True, as politicians they must be opportunists, must take half measures if they cannot get all. But as intelligent and liberal women they ought to realize that if the ballot is a weapon, the disinherited need it more than the economically superior class, and that the latter already enjoy too much power by virtue of their economic superiority.

The brilliant leader of the English suffragettes, Mrs. Emmeline Pankhurst, herself admitted, when on her American lecture tour, that there can be no equality between political superiors and inferiors. If so, how will the workingwoman of England, already inferior economically to the ladies who are benefited by the Shackleton bill,* be able to work with their political superiors, should the bill pass? Is it not probable that the class of Annie Keeney, so full of zeal, devotion and martyrdom, will be compelled to carry on their backs their female political bosses, even as they are carrying their economic masters. They would still have to do it, were universal suffrage for men and women established in England. No matter what the workers do, they are made to pay, always. Still, those who believe in the power of the vote show little sense of justice when they concern themselves not at all with those whom, as they claim, it might serve most.

The American suffrage movement has been, until very recently, altogether a parlor affair, absolutely detached from the economic needs of the people. Thus Susan B. Anthony, no doubt an exceptional type of woman, was not only indifferent, but antagonistic to labor; nor did she hesitate to manifest her antagonism when, in 1869, she advised women to take the places

---

* Mr. Shackleton was a labor leader. It is therefore self-evident that he should introduce a bill excluding his own constituents. The English Parliament is full of such Judases.

of striking printers in New York.* I do not know whether her attitude had changed before her death.

There are, of course, some suffragists who are affiliated with workingwomen—the Women's Trade Union League, for instance; but they are a small minority, and their activities are essentially economic. The rest look upon toil as a just provision of Providence. What would become of the rich, if not for the poor? What would become of these idle, parasitic ladies who squander more in a week than their victims earn in a year, if not for the eighty million wage workers? Equality, who ever heard of such a thing?

Few countries have produced such arrogance and snobbishness as America. Particularly this is true of the American woman of the middle class. She not only considers herself the equal of man, but his superior, especially in her purity, goodness and morality. Small wonder that the American suffragist claims for her vote the most miraculous powers. In her exalted conceit, she does not see how truly enslaved she is, not so much by man, as by her own silly notions and traditions. Suffrage cannot ameliorate that sad fact; it can only accentuate it, as indeed it does.

---

* *Equal Suffrage*, Dr. Helen A. Sumner

One of the great American women leaders claims that woman is entitled not only to equal pay, but that she ought to be legally entitled even to the pay of her husband. Failing to support her, he should be put in convict stripes and his earnings in prison be collected by his equal wife. Does not another brilliant exponent of the cause claim for woman that her vote will abolish the social evil, which has been fought in vain by the collective efforts of the most illustrious minds the world over? It is indeed to be regretted that the alleged creator of the universe has already presented us with his wonderful scheme of things, else woman suffrage would surely enable woman to outdo him completely.

Nothing is so dangerous as the dissection of a fetich. If we have outlived the time when such heresy was punishable at the stake, we have not outlived the narrow spirit of condemnation of those who dare differ with accepted notions. Therefore, I shall probably be put down as an opponent of woman. But that cannot deter me from looking the question squarely in the face. I repeat what I have said in the beginning: I do not believe that woman will make politics worse; nor can I believe that she could make it better. If, then, she cannot improve on man's mistakes, why perpetuate the latter?

History may be a compilation of lies; nevertheless, it contains a few truths, and they are the only guide we have for the future. The history of the political activities of men proves that they have given him absolutely nothing that he could not have achieved in a more direct, less costly, and more lasting manner. As a matter of fact, every inch of ground he has gained has been through a constant fight, a ceaseless struggle for self-assertion, and not through suffrage. There is no reason whatever to assume that woman, in her climb to emancipation, has been, or will be, helped by the ballot.

In the darkest of all countries, Russia, with her absolute despotism, woman has become man's equal, not through the ballot, but by her will to be and to do. Not only has she conquered for herself every avenue of learning and vocation, but she has won man's esteem, his respect, his comradeship; aye, even more than that: she has gained the admiration, the respect of the whole world. That, too, not through suffrage, but by her wonderful heroism, her fortitude, her ability, will power and her endurance in the struggle for liberty. Where are the women in any suffrage country or State that can lay claim to such a victory? When we consider the accomplishments of woman in America, we find also that something deeper and more powerful than suffrage has helped her in the march to emancipation.

It is just sixty-two years ago since a handful of women at the Seneca Falls Convention set forth a few demands for their right to equal education with men and access to the various professions, trades, etc. What wonderful accomplishment, what wonderful triumphs! Who but the most ignorant dare speak of woman as a mere domestic drudge? Who dare suggest that this or that profession should not be open to her? For over sixty years, she has molded a new atmosphere and a new life for herself. She has become a world power in every domain of human thought and activity. And all that without suffrage, without the right to make laws, without the "privilege" of becoming a judge, a jailer or an executioner.

Yes, I may be considered an enemy of woman; but if I can help her see the light, I shall not complain.

The misfortune of woman is not that she is unable to do the work of man, but that she is wasting her life force to outdo him, with a tradition of centuries which has left her physically incapable of keeping pace with him. Oh, I know some have succeeded, but at what cost, at what terrific cost! The import is not the kind of work woman does, but rather the quality of the work she furnishes. She can give suffrage or the ballot no new quality, nor can she receive anything from it that will enhance her own quality. Her development, her freedom, her independence, must come from and through herself. First, by asserting herself as a personality, and not as a sex commodity. Second, by refusing the right to anyone over her body; by refusing to bear children, unless she wants them; by refusing to be a servant to God, the State, society, the husband, the family, etc.; by making her life simpler, but deeper and richer. That is, by trying to learn the meaning and substance of life in all its complexities, by freeing herself from the fear of public opinion and public condemnation. Only that, and not the ballot, will set woman free, will make her a force hitherto unknown in the world, a force for real love, for peace, for harmony; a force of divine fire, of life giving; a creator of free men and women.

The Tragedy of Woman's Emancipation

Published in *Anarchism and Other Essays*, 1911

I BEGIN WITH an admission: Regardless of all political and economic theories, treating of the fundamental differences between various groups within the human race, regardless of class and race distinctions, regardless of all artificial boundary lines between woman's rights and man's rights, I hold that there is a point where these differentiations may meet and grow into one perfect whole.

With this, I do not mean to propose a peace treaty. The general social antagonism which has taken hold of our entire public life today, brought about through the force of opposing and contradictory interests, will crumble to pieces when the reorganization of our social life, based upon the principles of economic justice, shall have become a reality.

Peace or harmony between the sexes and individuals does not necessarily depend on a superficial equalization of human beings; nor does it call for the elimination of individual traits and peculiarities. The problem that confronts us today, and which the nearest future is to solve, is how to be one's self and yet in oneness with others, to feel deeply with all human beings and still retain one's own characteristic qualities. This seems to me to be the basis upon which the mass and the individual, the true democrat and the true individuality, man and woman, can meet without antagonism and opposition. The motto should not be: Forgive one another; rather: Understand one another. The oft-quoted sentence of Madame de Stael: "To understand everything means to forgive everything," has never particularly appealed to me; it has the odor of the confessional; to forgive one's fellow-being conveys the idea of pharisaical superiority. To understand one's fellow-being suffices. The admission partly represents the fundamental aspect of my views on the emancipation of woman and its effect upon the entire sex.

Emancipation should make it possible for woman to be human in the truest sense. Everything within her that craves assertion and activity should reach its fullest expression; all artificial barriers should be broken and the road towards greater freedom cleared of every trace of centuries of submission and slavery.

This was the original aim of the movement for woman's emancipation. But the results so far achieved have isolated woman and have robbed her of the fountain springs of that happiness which is so essential to her. Merely external emancipation has made of the modern woman an artificial being, who reminds one of the products of French arboriculture with its arabesque trees and shrubs, pyramids, wheels and wreaths; anything, except the forms which would be reached by the expression of her own inner qualities. Such artificially grown plants of the female sex are to be found in large numbers, especially in the so-called intellectual sphere of our life.

Liberty and equality for woman! What hopes and aspirations these words awakened when they were first uttered by some of the noblest and bravest souls of those days. The sun in all his light and glory was to rise upon a new world; in this world, woman was to be free to direct her own destiny—an aim certainly worthy of the great enthusiasm, courage, perseverance and ceaseless effort of the tremendous host of pioneer men and women, who staked everything against a world of prejudice and ignorance.

My hopes also move towards that goal, but I hold that the emancipation of woman, as interpreted and practically applied today, has failed to reach that great end. Now, woman is confronted with the necessity of emancipating herself from emancipation if she really desires to be free. This may sound paradoxical, but is, nevertheless, only too true.

What has she achieved through her emancipation? Equal suffrage in a few States. Has that purified our political life, as many well-meaning advocates predicted? Certainly not. Incidentally, it is really time that persons with plain, sound judgment should cease to talk about corruption in politics in a boarding-school tone. Corruption of politics has nothing to do with the morals, or the laxity of morals, of various political personalities. Its cause is altogether a material one. Politics is the reflex of the business and industrial world, the mottos of which are: "To take is more blessed than to give;" "buy cheap and sell dear;" "one soiled hand washes the other." There is no hope even that woman, with her right to vote, will ever purify politics.

Emancipation has brought woman economic equality with man; that is, she can choose her own profession and trade; but as her past and present physical training has not equipped her with the necessary strength to compete with man, she is often compelled to exhaust all her energy, use up her vitality, and strain every nerve in order to reach the market value. Very few ever succeed, for it is a fact that women teachers, doctors, lawyers, architects and engineers are neither met with the same confidence as their male colleagues, nor receive equal remuneration. And those that do reach that enticing equality generally do so at the expense of their physical and psychical well-being. As to the great mass of working girls and women, how much independence is gained if the narrowness and lack of freedom of the home is exchanged for the narrowness and lack of freedom of the factory, sweat-shop, department store or office? In addition is the burden which is laid on many women of looking after a "home, sweet home"—cold, dreary, disorderly, uninviting—after a day's hard work. Glorious independence! No wonder that hundreds of girls are willing to accept the first offer of marriage, sick and tired of their "independence" behind the counter, at the sewing or typewriting machine. They are just as ready to marry as girls of the middle class, who long to throw off the yoke of parental supremacy. A so-called independence which leads only to earning the merest subsistence is not so enticing, not so ideal, that one could expect woman to sacrifice everything for it. Our highly praised independence is, after all, but a slow process of dulling and stifling woman's nature, her love instinct and her mother instinct.

Nevertheless, the position of the working girl is far more natural and human than that of her seemingly more fortunate sister in the more cultured professional walks of life—teachers, physicians, lawyers, engineers, etc., who have to make a dignified, proper appearance, while the inner life is growing empty and dead.

The narrowness of the existing conception of woman's independence and emancipation; the dread of love for a man who is not her social equal; the fear that love will rob her of her freedom and independence; the horror that love or the joy of motherhood will only hinder her in the full exercise of her profession—all these together make of the emancipated modern woman a compulsory vestal, before whom life, with its great clarifying sorrows and its deep, entrancing joys, rolls on without touching or gripping her soul.

Emancipation, as understood by the majority of its adherents and exponents, is of too narrow a scope to permit the boundless love and ecstasy contained in the deep emotion of the true woman, sweetheart, mother, in freedom.

The tragedy of the self-supporting or economically free woman does not lie in too many but in too few experiences. True, she surpasses her sister of past generations in knowledge of the world and human nature; it is just because of this that she feels deeply the lack of life's essence, which alone can enrich the human soul, and without which the majority of women have become mere professional automatons.

That such a state of affairs was bound to come was foreseen by those who realized that, in the domain of ethics, there still remained many decaying ruins of the time of the undisputed superiority of man; ruins that are still considered useful. And, what is more important, a goodly number of the emancipated are unable to get along without them. Every movement that aims at the destruction of existing institutions and the replacement thereof with something more advanced, more perfect, has followers who in theory stand for the most radical ideas, but who, nevertheless, in their everyday practice, are like the average Philistine, feigning respectability and clamoring for the good opinion of their opponents. There are, for example, Socialists, and even Anarchists, who stand for the idea that property is robbery, yet who will grow indignant if anyone owe them the value of a half-dozen pins.

The same Philistine can be found in the movement for woman's emancipation. Yellow journalists and milk-and-water litterateurs have painted pictures of the emancipated woman that make the hair of the good citizen and his dull companion stand up on end. Every member of the woman's rights movement was pictured as a George Sand in her absolute disregard of morality. Nothing was sacred to her. She had no respect for the ideal relation between man and woman. In short, emancipation stood only for a reckless life of lust and sin; regardless of society, religion and morality. The exponents of woman's rights were highly indignant at such representation, and, lacking humor, they exerted all their energy to prove that they were not at all as bad as they were painted, but the very reverse. Of course, as long as woman was the slave of man, she could not be good and pure, but now that she was free and independent she would prove how good she could be and that her influence would have a purifying effect on all institutions in society. True, the movement for woman's rights has broken many old fetters, but it has also forged new ones. The great movement of TRUE emancipation has not met with a great race of women who could look liberty in the face. Their narrow, Puritanical vision banished man, as a disturber and doubtful character, out of their emotional life. Man was not to be tolerated at any price, except perhaps as the father of a child, since a child could not very well come to life without a father. Fortunately, the most rigid Puritans never will be strong enough to kill the innate craving for motherhood. But woman's freedom is closely allied with man's freedom, and many of my so-called emancipated sisters seem to overlook the fact that a child born in freedom needs the love and devotion of each human being about him, man as well as woman. Unfortunately, it is this narrow conception of human relations that has brought about a great tragedy in the lives of the modern man and woman.

About fifteen years ago appeared a work from the pen of the brilliant Norwegian, Laura Marholm, called *Woman, A Character Study*. She was one of the first to call attention to the emptiness and narrowness of the existing conception of woman's emancipation, and its tragic effect upon the inner life of woman. In her work, Laura Marholm speaks of the fate of several gifted women of international fame: the genius, Eleonora Duse; the great mathematician and writer, Sonya Kovalevskaia; the artist and poet-nature, Marie Bashkirtzeff, who died so young. Through each description of the lives of these women of such extraordinary mentality runs a marked trail of unsatisfied craving for a full, rounded, complete and beautiful life, and the unrest and loneliness resulting from the lack of it. Through these masterly psychological sketches, one cannot help but see that the higher the mental development of woman, the less possible it is for her to meet a congenial mate who will see in her, not only sex, but also the human being, the friend, the comrade and strong individuality, who cannot and ought not lose a single trait of her character.

The average man with his self-sufficiency, his ridiculously superior airs of patronage towards the female sex, is an impossibility for woman as depicted in the *Character Study* by Laura Marholm. Equally impossible for her is the man who can see in her nothing more than her mentality and her genius, and who fails to awaken her woman nature.

A rich intellect and a fine soul are usually considered necessary attributes of a deep and beautiful personality. In the case of the modern woman, these attributes serve as a hindrance to the complete assertion of her being. For over a hundred years, the old form of marriage, based on the Bible, "till death doth part," has been denounced as an institution that stands for the sovereignty of the man over the woman, of her complete submission to his whims and commands and absolute dependence on his name and support. Time and again it has been conclusively proved that the old matrimonial relation restricted woman to the function of a man's servant and the bearer of his children. And yet we find many emancipated women who prefer marriage, with all its deficiencies, to the narrowness of an unmarried life; narrow and unendurable because of the chains of moral and social prejudice that cramp and bind her nature.

The explanation of such inconsistency on the part of many advanced women is to be found in the fact that they never truly understood the meaning of emancipation. They thought that all that was needed was independence from external tyrannies; the internal tyrants, far more harmful to life and growth—ethical and social conventions—were left to take care of themselves; and they have taken care of themselves. They seem to get along as beautifully in the heads and hearts of the most active exponents of woman's emancipation, as in the heads and hearts of our grandmothers.

These internal tyrants, whether they be in the form of public opinion or what will mother say, or brother, father, aunt or relative of any sort; what will Mrs. Grundy, Mr. Comstock, the employer, the Board of Education say? All these busybodies, moral detectives, jailers of the human spirit, what will they say? Until woman has learned to defy them all, to stand firmly on her own ground and to insist upon her own unrestricted freedom, to listen to the voice of her nature, whether it call for life's greatest treasure, love for a man, or her most glorious privilege, the right to give birth to a child, she cannot call herself emancipated. How many emancipated women are brave enough to acknowledge that the voice of love is calling, wildly beating against their breasts, demanding to be heard, to be satisfied.

The French writer, Jean Reibrach, in one of his novels, *New Beauty*, attempts to picture the ideal, beautiful, emancipated woman. This ideal is embodied in a young girl, a physician. She talks very cleverly and wisely of how to feed infants; she is kind and administers medicines free to poor mothers. She converses with a young man of her acquaintance about the sanitary conditions of the future, and how various bacilli and germs shall be exterminated by the use of stone walls and floors, and by the doing away with rugs and hangings. She is, of course, very plainly and practically dressed, mostly in black. The young man, who, at their first meeting, was overawed by the wisdom of his emancipated friend, gradually learns to understand her, and recognizes one fine day that he loves her. They are young, and she is kind and beautiful, and though always in rigid attire, her appearance is softened by a spotlessly clean white collar and cuffs. One would expect that he would tell her of his love, but he is not one to commit romantic absurdities. Poetry and the enthusiasm of love cover their blushing faces before the pure beauty of the lady. He silences the voice of his nature and remains correct. She, too, is always exact, always rational, always well behaved. I fear if they had formed a union, the young man would have risked freezing to death. I must confess that I can see nothing beautiful in this new beauty, who is as cold as the stone walls and floors she dreams of. Rather would I have the love songs of romantic ages, rather Don Juan and Madame Venus, rather an elopement by ladder and rope on a moonlight night, followed by the father's curse, mother's moans, and the moral comments of neighbors, than correctness and propriety measured by yardsticks. If love does not know how to give and take without restrictions, it is not love, but a transaction that never fails to lay stress on a plus and a minus.

The greatest shortcoming of the emancipation of the present day lies in its artificial stiffness and its narrow respectabilities, which produce an emptiness in woman's soul that will not let her drink from the fountain of life. I once remarked that there seemed to be a deeper relationship between the old-fashioned mother and hostess, ever on the alert for the happiness of her little ones and the comfort of those she loved, and the truly new woman, than between the latter and her average emancipated sister. The disciples of emancipation pure and simple declared me a heathen, fit only for the stake. Their blind zeal did not let them see that my comparison between the old and the new was merely to prove that a goodly number of our grandmothers had more blood in their veins, far more humor and wit, and certainly a greater amount of naturalness, kind-heartedness and simplicity, than the majority of our emancipated professional women who fill the colleges, halls of learning and various offices. This does not mean a wish to return to the past, nor does it condemn woman to her old sphere, the kitchen and the nursery.

Salvation lies in an energetic march onward towards a brighter and clearer future. We are in need of unhampered growth out of old traditions and habits. The movement for woman's emancipation has so far made but the first step in that direction. It is to be hoped that it will gather strength to make another. The right to vote, or equal civil rights, may be good demands, but true emancipation begins neither at the polls nor in courts. It begins in woman's soul. History tells us that every oppressed class gained true liberation from its masters through its own efforts. It is necessary that woman learn that lesson, that she realize that her freedom will reach as far as her power to achieve her freedom reaches. It is, therefore, far more important for her to begin with her inner regeneration, to cut loose from the weight of prejudices, traditions and customs. The demand for equal rights in every vocation of life is just and fair; but, after all, the most vital right is the right to love and be loved. Indeed, if partial emancipation is to become a complete and true emancipation of woman, it will have to do away with the ridiculous notion that to be loved, to be sweetheart and mother, is synonymous with being slave or subordinate. It will have to do away with the absurd notion of the dualism of the sexes, or that man and woman represent two antagonistic worlds.

Pettiness separates; breadth unites. Let us be broad and big. Let us not overlook vital things because of the bulk of trifles confronting us. A true conception of the relation of the sexes will not admit of conqueror and conquered; it knows of but one great thing: to give of one's self boundlessly, in order to find one's self richer, deeper, better. That alone can fill the emptiness, and transform the tragedy of woman's emancipation into joy, limitless joy.

Marriage and Love

Published in *Anarchism and Other Essays*, 1911

THE POPULAR NOTION about marriage and love is that they are synonymous, that they spring from the same motives, and cover the same human needs. Like most popular notions, this also rests not on actual facts, but on superstition.

Marriage and love have nothing in common; they are as far apart as the poles; are, in fact, antagonistic to each other. No doubt, some marriages have been the result of love. Not, however, because love could assert itself only in marriage; much rather, is it because few people can completely outgrow a convention. There are today large numbers of men and women to whom marriage is naught but a farce, but who submit to it for the sake of public opinion. At any rate, while it is true that some marriages are based on love, and while it is equally true that, in some cases, love continues in married life, I maintain that it does so regardless of marriage, and not because of it.

On the other hand, it is utterly false that love results from marriage. On rare occasions, one does hear of a miraculous case of a married couple falling in love after marriage, but on close examination, it will be found that it is a mere adjustment to the inevitable. Certainly the growing-used to each other is far away from the spontaneity, the intensity, and beauty of love, without which the intimacy of marriage must prove degrading to both the woman and the man.

Marriage is primarily an economic arrangement, an insurance pact. It differs from the ordinary life insurance agreement only in that it is more binding, more exacting. Its returns are insignificantly small compared with the investments. In taking out an insurance policy, one pays for it in dollars and cents, always at liberty to discontinue payments. If, however, woman's premium is her husband, she pays for it with her name, her privacy, her self-respect, her very life, "until death doth part." Moreover, the marriage insurance condemns her to life-long dependency, to parasitism, to complete uselessness, individual as well as social. Man, too, pays his toll, but as his sphere is wider, marriage does not limit him as much as woman. He feels his chains more in an economic sense.

Thus Dante's motto over Inferno applies with equal force to marriage. "Ye who enter here leave all hope behind."

That marriage is a failure, none but the very stupid will deny. One has but to glance over the statistics of divorce to realize how bitter a failure marriage really is. Nor will the stereotyped Philistine argument that the laxity of divorce laws and the growing looseness of woman account for the fact that: first, every twelfth marriage ends in divorce; second, that since 1870 divorces have increased from 28 to 73 for every hundred thousand population; third, that adultery, since 1867, as ground for divorce, has increased 270.8 percent; fourth, that desertion increased 369.8 percent.

Added to these startling figures is a vast amount of material, dramatic and literary, further elucidating this subject. Robert Herrick, in *Together*; Pinero, in *Mid-Channel*; Eugene Walter, in *Paid In Full*, and scores of other writers are discussing the barrenness, the monotony, the sordidness, the inadequacy of marriage as a factor for harmony and understanding.

The thoughtful social student will not content himself with the popular superficial excuse for this phenomenon. He will have to dig deeper into the very life of the sexes to know why marriage proves so disastrous.

Edward Carpenter says that behind every marriage stands the life-long environment of the two sexes; an environment so different from each other that man and woman must remain strangers. Separated by an insurmountable wall of superstition, custom and habit, marriage has not the potentiality of developing knowledge of, and respect for, each other, without which every union is doomed to failure.

Henrik Ibsen, the hater of all social shams, was probably the first to realize this great truth. Nora leaves her husband, not—as the stupid critic would have it—because she is tired of her responsibilities or feels the need of woman's rights, but because she has come to know that for eight years she had lived with a stranger and borne him children. Can there be anything more humiliating, more degrading, than a life-long proximity between two strangers? No need for the woman to know anything of the man, save his income. As to the knowledge of the woman—what is there to know except that she has a pleasing appearance? We have not yet outgrown the theologic myth that woman has no soul, that she is a mere appendix to man, made out of his rib just for the convenience of the gentleman who was so strong that he was afraid of his own shadow.

Perchance the poor quality of the material whence woman comes is responsible for her inferiority. At any rate, woman has no soul—what is there to know about her? Besides, the less soul a woman has, the greater her asset as a wife, the more readily will she absorb herself in her husband. It is this slavish acquiescence to man's superiority that has kept the marriage institution seemingly intact for so long a period. Now that woman is coming into her own, now that she is actually growing aware of herself as being outside of the master's grace, the sacred institution of marriage is gradually being undermined, and no amount of sentimental lamentation can stay it.

From infancy, almost, the average girl is told that marriage is her ultimate goal; therefore her training and education must be directed towards that end. Like the mute beast fattened for slaughter, she is prepared for that. Yet, strange to say, she is allowed to know much less about her function as wife and mother than the ordinary artisan of his trade. It is indecent and filthy for a respectable girl to know anything of the marital relation. Oh, for the inconsistency of respectability that needs the marriage vow to turn something which is filthy into the purest and most sacred arrangement that none dare question or criticize. Yet that is exactly the attitude of the average upholder of marriage.

The prospective wife and mother is kept in complete ignorance of her only asset in the competitive field—sex. Thus she enters into life-long relations with a man only to find herself shocked, repelled, outraged beyond measure by the most natural and healthy instinct, sex. It is safe to say that a large percentage of the unhappiness, misery, distress and physical suffering of matrimony is due to the criminal ignorance in sex matters that is being extolled as a great virtue. Nor is it at all an exaggeration when I say that more than one home has been broken up because of this deplorable fact.

If, however, woman is free and big enough to learn the mystery of sex without the sanction of State or Church, she will stand condemned as utterly unfit to become the wife of a "good" man, his goodness consisting of an empty brain and plenty of money. Can there be anything more outrageous than the idea that a healthy, grown woman, full of life and passion, must deny nature's demand, must subdue her most intense craving, undermine her health and break her spirit, must stunt her vision, abstain from the depth and glory of sex experience until a "good" man comes along to take her unto himself as a wife? That is precisely what marriage means. How can such an arrangement end except in failure? This is one, though not the least important, factor of marriage, which differentiates it from love.

Ours is a practical age. The time when Romeo and Juliet risked the wrath of their fathers for love, when Gretchen exposed herself to the gossip of her neighbors for love, is no more. If, on rare occasions, young people allow themselves the luxury of romance, they are taken in care by the elders, drilled and pounded until they become "sensible."

The moral lesson instilled in the girl is not whether the man has aroused her love, but rather is it, "How much?" The important and only God of practical American life: Can the man make a living? can he support a wife? That is the only thing that justifies marriage. Gradually, this saturates every thought of the girl; her dreams are not of moonlight and kisses, of laughter and tears; she dreams of shopping tours and bargain counters. This soul poverty and sordidness are the elements inherent in the marriage institution. The State and Church approve of no other ideal, simply because it is the one that necessitates the State and Church control of men and women.

Doubtless, there are people who continue to consider love above dollars and cents. Particularly, this is true of that class whom economic necessity has forced to become self-supporting. The tremendous change in woman's position, wrought by that mighty factor, is indeed phenomenal when we reflect that it is but a short time since she has entered the industrial arena. Six million women wage workers; six million women, who have equal right with men to be exploited, to be robbed, to go on strike; aye, to starve even. Anything more, my lord? Yes, six million wage workers in every walk of life, from the highest brain work to the mines and railroad tracks; yes, even detectives and policemen. Surely the emancipation is complete.

Yet with all that, but a very small number of the vast army of women wage workers look upon work as a permanent issue in the same light as does man. No matter how decrepit the latter, he has been taught to be independent, self-supporting. Oh, I know that no one is really independent in our economic treadmill; still, the poorest specimen of a man hates to be a parasite; to be known as such, at any rate.

The woman considers her position as worker transitory, to be thrown aside for the first bidder. That is why it is infinitely harder to organize women than men. "Why should I join a union? I am going to get married, to have a home." Has she not been taught from infancy to look upon that as her ultimate calling? She learns soon enough that the home, though not so large a prison as the factory, has more solid doors and bars. It has a keeper so faithful that naught can escape him. The most tragic part, however, is that the home no longer frees her from wage slavery; it only increases her task.

According to the latest statistics submitted before a Committee "on labor and wages, and congestion of population," ten percent of the wage workers in New York City alone are married, yet they must continue to work at the most poorly paid labor in the world. Add to this horrible aspect the drudgery of housework, and what remains of the protection and glory of the home? As a matter of fact, even the middle-class girl in marriage cannot speak of her home, since it is the man who creates her sphere. It is not important whether the husband is a brute or a darling. What I wish to prove is that marriage guarantees woman a home only by the grace of her husband. There she moves about in *his* home, year after year, until her aspect of life and human affairs becomes as flat, narrow, and drab as her surroundings. Small wonder if she becomes a nag, petty, quarrelsome, gossipy, unbearable, thus driving the man from the house. She could not go if she wanted to; there is no place to go. Besides, a short period of married life, of complete surrender of all faculties, absolutely incapacitates the average woman for the outside world. She becomes reckless in appearance, clumsy in her movements, dependent in her decisions, cowardly in her judgment, a weight and a bore, which most men grow to hate and despise. Wonderfully inspiring atmosphere for the bearing of life, is it not?

But the child, how is it to be protected, if not for marriage? After all, is not that the most important consideration? The sham, the hypocrisy of it! Marriage protecting the child, yet thousands of children destitute and homeless. Marriage protecting the child, yet orphan asylums and reformatories overcrowded, the Society for the Prevention of Cruelty to Children keeping busy in rescuing the little victims from "loving" parents, to place them under more loving care, the Gerry Society. Oh, the mockery of it!

Marriage may have the power to bring the horse to water, but has it ever made him drink? The law will place the father under arrest and put him in convict's clothes; but has that ever stilled the hunger of the child? If the parent has no work, or if he hides his identity, what does marriage do then? It invokes the law to bring the man to "justice," to put him safely behind closed doors; his labor, however, goes not to the child, but to the State. The child receives but a blighted memory of his father's stripes.

As to the protection of the woman—therein lies the curse of marriage. Not that it really protects her, but the very idea is so revolting, such an outrage and insult on life, so degrading to human dignity, as to forever condemn this parasitic institution.

It is like that other paternal arrangement—capitalism. It robs man of his birthright, stunts his growth, poisons his body, keeps him in ignorance, in poverty, and dependence, and then institutes charities that thrive on the last vestige of man's self-respect.

The institution of marriage makes a parasite of woman, an absolute dependent. It incapacitates her for life's struggle, annihilates her social consciousness, paralyzes her imagination and then imposes its gracious protection, which is in reality a snare, a travesty on human character.

If motherhood is the highest fulfillment of woman's nature, what other protection does it need, save love and freedom? Marriage but defiles, outrages and corrupts her fulfillment. Does it not say to woman, Only when you follow me shall you bring forth life? Does it not condemn her to the block, does it not degrade and shame her if she refuses to buy her right to motherhood by selling herself? Does not marriage only sanction motherhood, even though conceived in hatred, in compulsion? Yet, if motherhood be of free choice, of love, of ecstasy, of defiant passion, does it not place a crown of thorns upon an innocent head and carve in letters of blood the hideous epithet, Bastard? Were marriage to contain all the virtues claimed for it, its crimes against motherhood would exclude it forever from the realm of love.

Love, the strongest and deepest element in all life, the harbinger of hope, of joy, of ecstasy; love, the defier of all laws, of all conventions; love, the freest, the most powerful moulder of human destiny; how can such an all-compelling force be synonymous with that poor little State and Church-begotten weed, marriage?

Free love? As if love is anything but free! Man has bought brains, but all the millions in the world have failed to buy love. Man has subdued bodies, but all the power on earth has been unable to subdue love. Man has conquered whole nations, but all his armies could not conquer love. Man has chained and fettered the spirit, but he has been utterly helpless before love. High on a throne, with all the splendor and pomp his gold can command, man is yet poor and desolate if love passes him by. And if it stays, the poorest hovel is radiant with warmth, with life and color. Thus love has the magic power to make of a beggar a king. Yes, love is free; it can dwell in no other atmosphere. In freedom it gives itself unreservedly, abundantly, completely. All the laws on the statutes, all the courts in the universe, cannot tear it from the soil, once love has taken root. If, however, the soil is sterile, how can marriage make it bear fruit? It is like the last desperate struggle of fleeting life against death.

Love needs no protection; it is its own protection. So long as love begets life, no child is deserted, or hungry, or famished for the want of affection. I know this to be true. I know women who became mothers in freedom by the men they loved. Few children in wedlock enjoy the care, the protection, the devotion free motherhood is capable of bestowing.

The defenders of authority dread the advent of a free motherhood, lest it will rob them of their prey. Who would fight wars? Who would create wealth? Who would make the policeman, the jailer, if woman were to refuse the indiscriminate breeding of children? The race, the race! shouts the king, the president, the capitalist, the priest. The race must be preserved, though woman be degraded to a mere machine—and the marriage institution is our only safety valve against the pernicious sex awakening of woman. But in vain, these frantic efforts to maintain a state of bondage. In vain, too, the edicts of the Church, the mad attacks of rulers, in vain even the arm of the law. Woman no longer wants to be a party to the production of a race of sickly, feeble, decrepit, wretched human beings, who have neither the strength nor moral courage to throw off the yoke of poverty and slavery. Instead she desires fewer and better children, begotten and reared in love and through free choice; not by compulsion, as marriage imposes. Our pseudo-moralists have yet to learn the deep sense of responsibility toward the child, that love in freedom has awakened in the breast of woman. Rather would she forego forever the glory of motherhood than bring forth life in an atmosphere that breathes only destruction and death. And if she does become a mother, it is to give to the child the deepest and best her being can yield. To grow with the child is her motto; she knows that in that manner alone can she help build true manhood and womanhood.

Ibsen must have had a vision of a free mother, when, with a master stroke, he portrayed Mrs. Alving. She was the ideal mother because she had outgrown marriage and all its horrors, because she had broken her chains and set her spirit free to soar until it returned a personality, regenerated and strong. Alas, it was too late to rescue her life's joy, her Oswald; but not too late to realize that love in freedom is the only condition of a beautiful life. Those who, like Mrs. Alving, have paid with blood and tears for their spiritual awakening, repudiate marriage as an imposition, a shallow, empty mockery. They know, whether love last but one brief span of time or for eternity, it is the only creative, inspiring, elevating basis for a new race, a new world.

In our present pygmy state, love is indeed a stranger to most people. Misunderstood and shunned, it rarely takes root; or if it does, it soon withers and dies. Its delicate fiber can not endure the stress and strain of the daily grind. Its soul is too complex to adjust itself to the slimy woof of our social fabric. It weeps and moans and suffers with those who have need of it, yet lack the capacity to rise to love's summit.

Someday, someday, men and women will rise, they will reach the mountain peak, they will meet big and strong and free, ready to receive, to partake, and to bask in the golden rays of love. What fancy, what imagination, what poetic genius can foresee even approximately the potentialities of such a force in the life of men and women. If the world is ever to give birth to true companionship and oneness, not marriage, but love will be the parent.

Born in Russia in 1869, EMMA GOLDMAN emigrated to the United States in 1885 to escape an arranged marriage. She soon found herself in the center of the various social activist movements pushing back against the plutocracy breaking the backs of workers across the U.S. and around the world.

Goldman became a highly sought-after lecturer on anarchist philosophy, women's rights, and social issues. Her sharp intellect and passion singled her out as a popular speaker; it was not uncommon for her events to draw thousands of listeners.

As her fame grew, so did her list of enemies—high society, wealthy industrialists, corrupt journalists, state and federal politicians. Goldman was arrested several times over the years for various reasons, including "inciting to riot" and illegally distributing information about birth control.

Eventually her activism led the U.S .Government to exile Goldman, along with Alexander Berkman and other dissidents, to Russia in 1921. Here she witnessed first-hand the brutality of the Communist experiment, which sparked her outspoken opposition to the Soviet regime.

Goldman was a prolific writer & publisher, founding the Mother Earth journal, and writing multiple pamphlets and articles for newspapers and magazines across the globe, as well as six books, including her expansive 2 volume memoir *Living My Life*, and the now-classic collection *Anarchism and Other Essays*.

Goldman spent the remainder of her life in exile from the U.S., living in various countries before eventually settling in Canada. She died in Toronto in 1940.

OTHER BOOKS BY VERTVOLTA PRESS

THE GROWING DISCONTENT OF THE MASSES:
Three Essays on the Social Condition, by EMMA GOLDMAN
978-1-60944-139-5

ANARCHISM AND OTHER ESSAYS, by EMMA GOLDMAN
978-1-60944-113-5

READYING TO RISE: *Essays* by MARCUS HARRISON GREEN
978-1-60944-143-2

EMERALD REFLECTIONS: *A* South Seattle Emerald *Anthology*
edited by MARCUS HARRISON GREEN
978-1-60944-109-8

EMERALD REFLECTIONS 2: *A* South Seattle Emerald *Anthology*
edited by MARCUS HARRISON GREEN
978-1-60944-132-6

Coming Soon

LIVING MY LIFE: A MEMOIR *Complete and Unabridged Edition*
by EMMA GOLDMAN
978-1-60944-141-8

www.vertvoltapress.com

www.ingramcontent.com/pod-product-compliance
Lightning Source LLC
Chambersburg PA
CBHW031154020426
42333CB00013B/657